Hillman Street High Roller

Hillman Street High Roller

Tales from a Belfast Boyhood

Sam McAughtry

Appletree Press

Published by
The Appletree Press Ltd
19-21 Alfred Street
Belfast BT2 8DL
1994

A catalogue record for this book is available from the British Library

ISBN 0 86281 446 4

9 8 7 6 5 4 3 2 1

Contents

Losing the Lot

*M*y love for a flutter on the horses goes back to the heart of my childhood days: back so far that I can recall a time when I imagined that real horse racing took place inside the bookie's office. Although I knew full well that it was impossible, I still believed that inside that place there was a long rail, beyond which was the racetrack, green and oval with a white fence enclosing it. The customers stood at the rail, watching and cheering their fancies, as the horses raced on magic turf that lay outside the limitations of reality, on the far side of the bookies. In fact, I was probably the first person in the world to foresee colour TV racing.

To the outsider's eye the pitch itself was a dreary enough sight on Halliday's Road, near to Tiger's Bay and Duncairn Gardens — a makeshift shed of a place in what was once a stable yard. By a margin of a good many years I was too young to be allowed in there. Indeed, I'll tell you how young I was — my adored brother Mart, later to die in World War Two, was seven years my senior, and yet he wasn't allowed in there either. But he had connections in that magic place. In the hot summer days of my sixth year, when he was thirteen and close to leaving school, he would sit beside me on the step by the door to the bookies, study the racing pages, write his selections on the back of a Park Drive packet and send in the bet, care of the next passing customer.

He was good at sorting out the form was Mart, but he was too hefty a punter. Mart worked after school hours as a message boy for a grocer on the Cavehill Road and for this he was paid two shillings a week. This represented a quarter of a week's rent for our kitchen house, so it wasn't buttons, and it was appreciated by Mother. But once or twice he had had to touch the heights of greatness in order to bet his way out of disaster; with the two shillings reduced by seven eighths to threepence, Mart would be looking frantically for someone with another threepenny bit to go in with him in a desperation sixpenny double. It said a lot for his professionalism that, in these circumstances, he didn't go for two low-priced favourites just to get the original two shillings back. Oh no.

"To hell with it," Mart would say, "we deserve the suffering money. Let's look for something to bump up the odds," and down he would get to the study of a hard handicap, a cavalry charge over the sprint distance. With astonishing regularity Mart would pull if off and present our delighted mother with four shillings instead of two; my hero walking carefully, so that the rest of the silver winnings wouldn't chink in his trouser pocket.

So it was my love for Mart that helped make horse racing a happy scene for me. Another thing that helped was the smell of pipe tobacco and Woodbines that hung about the pitch on Halliday's Road. My father smoked the pipe when he was broke and Woodbines when he wasn't. So, although Dad had no interest in the bookies, its smell was his smell when, on his arrival home, just paid off from his ship, he would pick me up and hold me close and kiss me and give me what he called a grizzly hug and surround me in gorgeous, passive smoke.

In later years Mart and Dad served on the same ship. Once, when I was fifteen and Mart was twenty two, the ship paid off in the morning, so Mart and I were in the bookies in time for the first race. He'd slipped me five shillings on the way up Hillman Street and this I clutched tightly in my pocket. I wasn't about to bet with it because Mart was in action and I didn't want to stop any of his selections, either by backing the same ones or by betting against him.

He would stand talking sport with his friends in the bookies between races. Mart was popular: he was a good loser and generous to his out-of-work mates when he had a bit of money. Just home from sea, with maybe two months' money in his pocket, his bets were on the big side and just about everybody in the place wanted him to win, except, of course, the bookie.

And this day the bookie's wish came true. Mart started off losing, kept it up, took the head staggers, plunged and lost the lot.

We walked in silence, the two of us, back down Hillman Street at half past four. Well, not quite in silence: Mart was whistling tunelessly; I was crying inside for him.

He was going with a girl at the time and she was at that moment sitting at her machine in the wareroom hemstitching

9

shirts, probably stitching them all wrong and fastening the tails to the front so all aglow was she, not knowing that our Mart had lost the lot, that the marriage fund was at a standstill until the next trip.

When he was slipping money to a deserving case, Mart did it by reaching, arms down, for the other's hand and closing the man's fingers around the cash. "That'll get you a drink," he would say. That's how he gave it to me and I'd seen him do it a hundred times to shipmates stranded ashore.

As we walked down Hillman Street, I stopped his right hand from swinging and closed his fingers around the five shillings he'd given me.

"That'll take you and Maggie out tonight," I said gruffly, in seamanlike fashion.

He turned as we walked and looked at me. I didn't look back at him. I didn't want to see if he was smiling. I was burning red.

"Thanks," he said.

In all the fifty odd years since that day I've done lots of things that pleased me, but not one of them gave me as much pleasure as being able to give Mart the five shillings, the day he lost the lot.

Honesty Always Pays

When we were kids running about Cosgrave Street and Mackey Street and all up and down the Limestone Road, we always had to keep an eye out for Fairy Feet. He was the local cop, a huge man, with a face like a bannock and hands like shovels. Here's a tale to show how Fairy Feet was regarded round our way.

One winter's day, when thick snow lay on the ground, the Reverend Dr Johnston of Newington Presbyterian Church was strolling up the Limestone Road. Dr Johnston was a temperance leader, nicknamed Pussyfoot by the vintners because he was always saying that, where drink was concerned, he wasn't going to pussyfoot around. He was feeling good this day, the air was crisp and dry and he was heading for the Manse and a good meal, followed no doubt with a milk chaser. Glorying in his rumbling stomach, the clergyman raised his eyes to heaven – only to see, on top of the ten-foot wall that surrounded a disused brickworks, a group of local men pissed to the eyeballs, loaded to the gills with Chateau Garmoyle Street 1935, more commonly known as blowy-up.

They hailed the Reverend Doctor in a friendly manner with

greetings like, "What about ye, oul hand," and "Does yer mother know yer out?" The man of the cloth wasn't in the least put out by this. He liked the common man. He stopped and spread his gaitered legs, then he narrowed his eyes and peered up with new interest. No wonder, because balanced on the wall between the men was a giant snowball, fully six feet in diameter.

How they had managed to hoist the thing up onto the wall was a matter for the minister to speculate upon later, but for the present he asked, "What are you going to do with that, might I ask?"

"We're going to keep it up here till it's dark," he was told.

"With what object?"

He wasn't long in learning with what object.

"It's in the dark that Fairy Feet walks up here."

"Yes, well?"

"Well, when he reaches where you've reached, we're going to drop it on his head."

It took a hell of a lot to render Dr Johnston speechless, but, for fully five seconds, he was stunned – then, "But, if that lands on the constable's head it'll . . . Why, it'll drive him into the ground like a nail."

The men of Tiger's Bay grinned in appreciation, "We know."

The minister of Newington Presbyterian Church shook his fist.

"Strong drink is a mocker," he shouted.

"It might be a mocker, but it's hard to whack for putting the time in," one of them called, pulling a bottle of red biddy from his pocket, and the Reverend moved on, excited all to hell's gates by the only thing that ever excites a clergyman – a theme for his sermon on Sunday. It would be "What soberness conceals, drunkenness reveals (Latin proverb)."

For the record, that night Fairy Feet made it safely up the Limestone Road without being compressed into a dwarf seven foot broad. He changed his routine and walked up the other side. That's the kind of operator he was. We used to say that he was like a fly, with a hundred eyes.

The big peeler's speciality was to leap out of absolutely nowhere right into the middle of unsuspecting card schools. These schools attracted the unemployed men. Their dole had been cut by the government: indeed, in many cases they got no dole at all unless they were willing to work for buttons, drawing Outdoor Relief for concreting the streets. So the card school was a kind of magic carpet by which, if the cards fell right, a man might win the full of his arms of good grub for his family, not to mention the ecstasy of sinking enough drink for him to jap his brains out on a handy lamppost.

Most of the men who played cards had fought in the trenches. The war was only a matter of ten years won and there were still signs of it everywhere. At the doors were children's swings made of the canvas webbing that the men had worn in France, and hanging in many a hall would be a tin hat with green leaves trailing from it. On the street every now and then would appear the casualties of the war. Some of them were shy of a limb, others were mustard gas cases coughing their lungs away, and of course there were our friends the shell-shocked, holding their sticks like rifles,

13

shouting at nobody, in a language that nobody understood. It's a curious thing that if a man was born with a bit of a want in him in those times, the kids all made fun of him. An example of this was plump, ginger-haired, forty-year-old Johnny Butternut, real name unknown. He had the giggle of a toddler, innocent eyes and a very spittley mouth, and that's all. But the kids of the street gave him hardly any peace, making mockery of him for as long as he was in the area. Nobody ever laughed at the shell-shock cases though, and they did more outlandish things than Johnny Butternut ever did.

One of them, with wild staring eyes, would make machine gun noises as he made his way along the street; another would suddenly stop, look up at the sky and run for cover in the nearest doorway. These casualties included some men who, by their dress and their voices, were clearly of a higher class than ourselves and it could have been because of this that, in a strange way, shell-shock behaviour, however bizarre, was regarded with tolerance.

But Fairy Feet now, he didn't regard anything with tolerance. He was single-minded, a machine for lifting people. It was all the same to him if he was lifting ten-year-old me, as he did, and having me fined half a crown for playing football in the street, or lifting one of the men that he saw congregating at the street corner. Congregating was a crime. When Fairy Feet appeared, the congregation dispersed. That's if he gave them time. Sometimes he would slip down a back entry, go through somebody's house, leap out of a front door and lift a random sample before the congregation even knew he was there.

The big peeler thought he was into a red-letter day when he managed to gain access through Mrs McCusker's house on the Limestone Road and burst out of her back door, into the common entry with Cosgrave Street, onto a bit of waste ground and clean on top of a banker school that comprised a good dozen men.

Banker is a game that has all but disappeared. Maybe it was too simple to stand up to the sophisticated times to come. It was rudimentary in fact, but it had its strong adherents sixty years ago because of its simplicity and sheet lightning outcome.

One man ran the bank. He set out the required number of cards face down and the punters backed their fancy. The banker covered the bets, with one card left for the banker, and when all bets were on and covered and the cards were turned face up, only those higher in value than the banker's were winners. Nobody needed a PhD to play banker; it wasn't even necessary to have a poker face. A man could lose his wages in minutes at it. Indeed, I saw Winston Jackson, nicknamed Paul Robeson because he was an albino, lose his firewood round, pony and all, to a guy called Big Leachy in a matter of fifteen minutes.

To counter Fairy Feet, every strong banker school posted lookouts. Keeping dick, it was called. This was a job for kids because they could look so innocent and it paid well, tuppence a time for maybe two hours sentry go.

This wasn't without its perils: some of the lookouts were stationed on top of back yard walls. The lavatory was in the yard and, when the women felt the need to go to the yard, they didn't take kindly to having wee boys up on the wall watching. Especially since, if it was a quick job, the half of the time the women didn't bother using the lavatory at all.

On the day that Fairy Feet pulled off his coup, I was one of those keeping dick. I was on a wall beside Mrs McCusker's. Just before he reached the back door in a dark green blur I spotted him and gave the shout "Fairy Feet!", before tight-rope running along the tops of the back yard walls to safety.

In the space of a millisecond there were just a dozen scuffs of dirt where the men had once stood. Provision had been made for this. Big Leachy lived alone: his house backed onto the waste ground and the back door was open and handy as an escape route.

In one second flat, the whole banker school was through it, the door was barred and the men were in Big Leachy's kitchen, breathing hard. But unfortunately the alarm had come too late to save the money. The bets had been covered and the dough, a good couple of quid, was down on the ground beside the cards.

By the time that Fairy Feet emerged onto Cosgrave Street, my mate Frankie Pattison and I were innocently standing, rhyming off the thirty two counties of Ireland, letting on that we were doing our school homework.

With his red moon face beaming, the constable came out of the entry. He had the money and the cards rolled up in his hanky and he was swinging the hanky jauntily as he walked.

"Antrim, Armagh, Down, Fermanagh, Londonderry and

Tyrone," we chanted, Frankie and I, as Fairy Feet passed us with hardly a glance, humming to himself with satisfaction. He swung the hanky back and forth with each step that he took. At the same time with his other hand he made to reach into his tunic pocket, probably to get his notebook out prior to recording the details of his magnificent achievement. But this proved to be a major mistake.

The co-ordination needed to do this would have been money for jam for any normal person, but for Fairy Feet, whose brain and nerves and reflexes had been fashioned by the Lord for only the one purpose – lifting people – it upset his way of going. He fumbled with the button, thought that he would bring the other hand into play and when he did, he only succeeded in letting go of the hanky full of money. And as the precious bundle hit the deck, it fell right at the feet of Mills Bomb McGrath, who happened to be passing at the time.

Mills Bomb was one of our more interesting shell-shock cases. He didn't cower down with his hands over his ears and he didn't aim his stick at snipers, nor did he fire off silent rounds at invisible German aeroplanes. What he did was to bend down suddenly, pick up any object of the rough size of a Mills bomb that he might come across, hurl it as far away from him as he could and turn and run like hell.

While Fairy Feet was trying to get his functions together, working out how to disengage his fingers from his tunic button, Mills Bomb swooped; the hanky and its contents soared into the air, right over our heads and landed clean smack into Big Leachy's back yard.

17

We saw it, Frankie Pattison and I, and I suppose Mills Bomb McGrath saw it, but his poor head wasn't up to retaining that sort of information. The thing is, Fairy Feet didn't see where the money had landed. He had only just managed to work out two things: one, that he was no longer in possession of the banker money and two, that Mills Bomb McGrath was legging it up the street like a scalded cat.

The bluebottle took off in chase and when Mills Bomb saw over his shoulder what looked like a huge German Feldwebel galloping after him, he put a foot or so onto his step and in no time at all the street was clear of police and shell-shock cases.

Frankie Pattison and I were left looking at each other. Frankie was still automatically rattling off Irish counties. I interrupted him at Cavan and Clare with a plan.

We knocked Big Leachy's door. There was no answer. The banker school had filtered through and escaped to freedom as the drama we had witnessed was taking place outside. I nodded to Frankie, we went round the back, I shinned up the wall, dropped into Big Leachy's yard and found the loot on top of the rubbish in the midden. Then I climbed back and we made for Martha McDevitt's sweet shop toot sweet, as the ex-soldiers said.

Loaded with caramels, ice-cream and Woodbine cigarettes, we rounded up the other three lookouts – Jamesie Moore, Bobby McCandless and Butler Forsythe – looked into their shining eyes and gave each a sixpenny piece, three times the going rate, five Woodbine and the full of their insides of sweets and ice-cream.

An hour later, nearly smoked and gorged to death, we threw the hanky and the cards and money back over Big Leachy's yard wall, then we went to his front door and knocked. The card school was back inside, looking glum.

"We just thought we would tell you that Fairy Feet dropped the banker money wrapped in his hanky and Mills Bomb McGrath threw it over your yard wall. Fairy Feet didn't see where it went," we said, dead out of breath and all virtue and purity.

They turned and ran together, jamming themselves in the scullery door like characters in a Mack Sennett comedy. Frankie and I were in the kitchen when they came back with the money. It was Big Leachy who opened the hanky and did the counting.

He looked at the others, "There's five shillings missing, would you believe it?"

They looked at each other, shaking their heads sadly.

"Talk about corruption in high places," said Gunner Gordon, who had just come out after doing a month for shoplifting. "It's enough to make you lose all confidence in the police."

"We could have knocked the lot off, Frankie and me, and said nothing," I said, "but we didn't, sure we didn't Frankie?"

"Here, take that tuppence each," said Big Leachy, "and here's another penny apiece. Your honesty is most refreshing."

The Master Story-teller

On a summer's evening the Cosgrave Street kids used to take themselves up to a man-made cave in which were old kilns, almost the last traces of a worked-out brickworks that used to sit on the north side of the Limestone Road. This was in the early Thirties, a time of high unemployment and a time of hunger unknown today to anyone under fifty. I can still remember my father returning home shortly after leaving our house to visit his sister on the New Lodge Road.

"What has you back so soon?" Mother asked.

He shrugged, "When I got to Lily's house, I could smell bacon frying and I didn't want to embarrass her."

Men who had survived the trenches in the First War gathered by the kilns to play cards or pitch and toss, or just to congregate, to kill the time, where there were no police to move them along.

There was nearly always a card school going — banker or pontoon or brag — these being simple games, where death was sudden. Belfastmen didn't, at that time, go in for thoughtful, drawn-out bluffing games like poker. It is likely that the quick in-and-out card games were favoured because, in the streets, the police swooped and the men scattered like lightning. If cash had to be left lying then it made sense to lose the product of just three minutes' gambling, instead of ten minutes' browsing and a hefty poke, as with poker.

Alongside the men's card school there would have been one for the schoolboys, with halfpenny stakes. The kids copied the men, "Come on, hurry up and cut the cards. And cut them deep, for a deep cut's a sore cut."

Over in another corner of the kilns there was always a group of wee boys who hadn't a lot of interest in playing cards. For me this was the cosiest corner of the cave, for this was where the talking and the story-telling went on. Cards were interesting, and at times even exciting, but experience had taught me that to stand close and watch was to prove the truth of John Donne's famous saying that no man is an island. Sooner or later a wiped-out gambler would put the bite on the nearest spectator, "Lend us a couple of dee, go on. My luck's bound to turn." Responses like "Away and bunt. I didn't get where I am today by hitting pasteboard with money," were a recipe for broken friendships, as I had already found out. So, apart from the high drama of a whole shilling going down on a hand of banker or something equally impressive, I was to be found away from the gambling, hunkered down and listening to tales of ghosts and banshees, to war stories handed down from our fathers, or − the biggest treat of all − a performance from our very own crown prince of story-tellers, Blow Kennedy.

Blow was small, dark like a gypsy, and, to us, a little mysterious. He lived with an old aunt, just the two of them, in a house on North Queen Street. The house had no lino, no paint on the walls and no beds. The two of them slept on a collection of old coats on the floor, in front of the fire. They would go out together on some sort of mission every morning, arriving home in the early afternoon. Some said that they went begging on the other side of town, but none of us had ever asked Blow about this side of his life, and he didn't mention it. Coming right down to it, we weren't interested; we loved his wonderful stories.

In particular, I was fond of his poetry, but here is a typical opening to one of Blow Kennedy's stories, a tale of the Wild West:

"Bang! bang! bang! Three shots rang out on the still night air. Three outlaws died in an instant. Three horses ran riderless through a clump of cottonwool trees. Ben Brody calmly bolstered his smoking revolver. 'The West is a cleaner place, Crazy Horse,' he said quietly, but Ben's faithful Indian companion was nowhere to be seen. He was over amongst the cottonwool trees, scalping the outlaws as hard as he could lick. Ben Brody smiled in the darkness, 'Aha,' he hissed in perfect English."

There was more. There was as much as we wanted. Blow Kennedy needed only to read a story once and he could repeat it, more or less as it appeared on the page.

Listening to him, the murmur of talk from the card schools faded to nothing and we were on Blow Kennedy's magic carpet, up in the clouds, high over Belfast's grey, slate acres, carried away to a world of his choosing. Sometimes it was fiction, sometimes history, sometimes news; it all depended on the content of whatever book or magazine or newspaper he chose to retrieve, in his own more-or-less style.

I'll never forget the expression on the face of an English teacher in the old Biroo School, the Ministry of Labour school for the unemployed in Alfred Street, the first time he encountered Blow Kennedy's singular talent. Each new lad to arrive at the school was given a test. "What would you like to do when you are a man?" was one of the questions in a literacy paper.

"I'm gone to rite bout history," wrote Blow, "in fect Iv aready started . . . " and he went on to quote a long slab lifted from Lord Macaulay's version of the Battle of the Boyne.

I took my test along with Blow that afternoon. I could hardly do my own work for reading over his shoulder and, when the work was handed in, I watched for the teacher's reaction, getting ready to save it up for the kilns later.

"This is the worst spelling I have ever seen in my life . . ." the teacher began. He was a young man who had recently graduated from Queen's University and was awaiting a position more suited to his talents than the Biroo School.

If there was such a substance as the essence of poverty, the concentrated distillation of want, this was where it was to be found. The very smell of it hung over the Alfred Street classrooms, an invisible haze, inverting the atmosphere, weighing down on all within. This particular teacher made no secret of his distaste for the place and for those who sailed in it.

". . . Yet . . . ," he continued, "yet, this whole work has an uncanny, inexplicable fascination." Blow, who'd been asked to stand up, blushed with pride.

"Take that essay home with you," I called out, "and read it alongside Macaulay's *History of England*." It was old stuff to me.

The teacher looked at me, nodded, and by next morning was a member of the Blow Kennedy fan club. The spelling was disastrous, words were subject to mysterious changes and the entire work seemed to be expelled in one breath, but the end result was riveting, and there was no denying the quality of the recall. Another thing: it was far more entertaining than the 1849 version, especially those references to the forces of King James who were called, in the Blow Kennedy version, Left Footers.

"I would find a place for you in the Tech. English evening classes," the teacher said next morning, "but I feel that education would snuff out something that can only be described as uniquely engaging. You should be the subject of a protection order."

"Do you want to hear the story of Eleanor Troy?" Blow asked delighted, "It's a well-known Greek Legion."

"I don't half," the teacher said . . .

Once, a newcomer to the kilns, a guy up from the country and a cousin of Butler Forsythe, snorted and began to correct Blow Kennedy's version of the story of Ben Brody. He stopped Blow in mid-flow.

"There's no such thing as a cottonwool tree," he said, "and another thing – revolvers are holstered, not bolstered."

Blow looked to the company for assistance. He was clearly knocked out of his stride. I took over. I spoke severely to the newcomer, "What's your name?"

"Walter McAdoo. There's no such thing as a cotton-wool . . ."

"Wait a minute, Walter McAdoo," I said. "Just answer me this: can you tell stories?"

"No, but if I could, I would tell them right."

I looked around at my companions. They nodded together, satisfied. They knew what was coming.

"Do your trick Blow," I said.

The master story-teller took a deep breath and began. He reeled off the books of the Bible in order, followed this with the thirty two counties of Ireland, listed in their most recent placings the teams in the Irish soccer league and recited the alphabet backwards. But this was only to lubricate his pipes. Starting at Fortwilliam Park, he named every street on the Antrim Road going towards the city centre, then he listed the tram route numbers and destinations for the entire Corporation network, mentioned thirty plant varieties and only stopped on the raising of my hand, as he was delivering the up-to-date list of heavyweight champions since James J Corbett in 1892.

I turned to Walter McAdoo. "Can you do that?" I asked.

He shook his head in awed silence.

"Is there such a thing as a cottonwool tree?"

He nodded.

"What do you do with a smoking revolver?"

"You bolster it."

"Exactly."

"Would you like to hear a poem?" Blow's eyes were shining. He knew how much it pleased me.

25

"If you would," Walter McAdoo said humbly.

"A slumber did my spirit steal,
I had no human fears,
She seemed a thing that could not feel
The touch of early tears;
No motion has she now, no corpse,
She neither hears nor sneezes,
Birled round in earth internal course,
With rocks and stones and treeses."

Blow Kennedy took our applause with becoming modesty. "That's about a wee girl called Lucy," he said. "She got knocked down or something. It was wrote by Woolworth."

The Case of the Cut Currant Cake

The times when honesty is the best policy are few and far between and this applies particularly to women. There are really only three questions to which a woman truly wants honest answers: the first is when she's asking a likely prospect if he's married, the second is when, having married him, she's asking him upwards of a year later if he's having an affair, and the third is when she's asking which one of her kids stole a collop off the cake.

The Greek philosopher Plato believed that poetry should be banned, because it was cutting the people off from the truth. In fact, his strictures applied to the whole of literature and children weren't given any dispensation either. Plato felt that it was wrong to tell them stories that contained any element of fiction. It follows that he must have felt the same way about the other side of the coin – when children told tales that contained an element of fiction to their parents.

Plato would have felt very uncomfortable if he'd seen the way that honesty was handled in our house when I was a lad. Which brings us to question number three above.

My mother baked this huge cake in aid of St Barnabas Church. It was a lovely cake, and it was baked for the Lord.

With Dad away at sea, the man of the house in our house was the Lord.

Hanging on our kitchen wall was that notice about the Lord being the Head of This House and the Unseen Guest at Our Table, although how He managed to find room at our table with seven of us sitting there already was hard to work out. Maybe He was sitting with His dinner on His lap on our sofa.

But in matters pertaining to the church, well, our whole family was available as a packet deal to the Lord for His disposal. We were there on Sunday at early Holy Communion at half past eight, morning Sunday school at ten o'clock, morning prayer at half past eleven, Brotherhood service for men only at two o'clock, afternoon Sunday school at three o'clock and evening service at seven. In between, it was hell's own job for me to fit in a couple of hands of poker at a school that ran all day at the foot of Mackey Street.

It was one of Mother's proudest moments to sit in church in the summer break and listen to the Rector, the Reverend R Dixon Patterson, call out our names amongst the winners of the prizes for Sunday school attendance. One after the other the McAughtrys were honoured. Mother's cheeks bloomed rose red as, in front of a packed church, we walked up to receive the Rector's handshake and prizes for First Class Attendance at morning and afternoon Sunday school.

We had a choice between the Bible and fiction; for me it was no contest: I went for G A Henty's adventure stories every time. The first thing I did when I got home was to write on the flyleaf, "This book is the property of Captain Sam McAughtry. Not To Be Removed!!!"

Once, just to see if it could be done, I mitched morning church and sat reading the *News of the World* in Alexandra Park. But it was too easy, not in the least as dicey as mitching school. Later that Sunday, over lunch, Mother asked me what the sermon was about.

"Something to do with God," I said, stealing a glance to where the Unseen Guest was sitting on the sofa. I was feeling more uneasy than I'd ever felt in my life before. I wasn't in line for a G A Henty for attendance at the Honesty school and that was for sure.

In the matter of the cake, honesty got a black eye very early. That cake had been baked using good fresh eggs, except that Mother thought they were cheap cracked ones. I'd been told to get cracked eggs for baking, but I forgot. The grocer gave me fresh eggs and charged them up. When I was just outside the house I suddenly remembered, so I sat down at the edge of the pavement, took out each egg and gently cracked it against the granite kerbstone. Then I went in and handed them to Mother.

"There you are," I said, "every one recently cracked."

She thanked me and said I was a good boy, wondering the while I suppose why my face was shining with good intent, truth and honesty.

There was good butter in that cake and currants and nuts, and when it was in the oven baking the smell filled the whole house, flooding the senses and agitating the taste buds, leading us to coax and cajole Mother to cut a collop off the cake before handing it over to the church.

"Who ever heard of a cake in a sale of work having a collop

cut out of it?" she wanted to know.

"If you use a good sharp knife you could cut four collops out of it, keeping the middle where it is, until it looks like a petal and display it as a petal cake. You'll probably win a prize for inventing a new shape of cake."

But it was no good. That cake would be seen by hundreds and it would be a cake, a whole cake, and nothing but a cake, so we were warned to keep our hands off the finished article until it was collected by a representative of the Mothers' Union the next day.

We were put to bed with the usual supper of bread and marge with a slice of elder on top. For those who don't know what elder is, it's lining from in or about the cow's udder. This we had to learn from outside sources, because in our house when we asked where elder came from, we were ignored and when we asked the second time, we were given a fourpenny one around the ear. So much for the pursuit of truth.

We crept like snails upstairs to bed, thinking about the cake. Bread and marge and elder were no substitute, we kids agreed lying there in the candlelight, three of us in the one bed and the other on a mattress on the floor. We decided to put one final argument to Mother. I was chosen to shout it down the stairs,

"You could cut a quarter collop off and give it to us, then divide the rest up into three triangles and say to the church, 'There. I'm giving you three cakes, specially shaped as triangles.'"

"If you don't keep quiet and go to sleep, you'll end up

specially shaped as a triangle," she yelled up the stairs and that's the way it was when night fell.

Next morning we were fed and watered and packed off to school.

When we came home it was to find an atmosphere of crisis. The woman from the Mothers' Union had called, Mother had taken the cake out, only to find that a huge collop had been cut out of it.

"Talk about a showing-up," Mother said, as she dropped our afternoon meal in front of us from a great height. "I wouldn't be surprised but what they'll expel me from the Mothers' Union. Right, who did it? Who cut the collop off the cake?"

There was only the sound of silence. Honesty right then would have been next door to suicidal.

"If you don't tell me I'll keep the lot of you in," she said.

No reply. She didn't really expect one: this was only the opening skirmish. So the four of us were placed under house arrest.

Later, at teatime, Mother tried another tack, "I'll tell your father when he comes home. You'll get no money from him."

This threat was emptier than last Saturday night's porter bottles. She had never ratted on us to Dad in her life and she wasn't about to start then. We said nothing.

For her next trick, Mother played the good cop, "All right," she said, "tell me who did it and I won't lift my hand."

As she spoke, she eyed the cane that hung on the wall. I gave a sigh. We had reached a familiar and final stage in the search for honesty.

"I did it!" I yelled, diving for safety.

"I'll have your sacred life!" Mother cried, grabbing the cane and sending it whistling through the air inches from the seat of my pants. But I made it to the street in overdrive.

An hour later I slipped quietly into the house again, to find the whole family, Mother included, giggling over the case of the cut currant cake.

That was the Tiger's Bay method of handling honesty. The route and the reasoning might have been too much for Plato, but if I had to put a defence to him I would offer as a plea bargain his own saying that a good poor man is better than a good rich man because the poor man has to resist more temptations. And by God that currant cake put Adam and Eve in the ha'penny place.

The Story of Isobel Bailey

There is an impression held today about the pre-war bottom layer generation that we had very little work to go to. This was true as far as adults were concerned in the late Twenties and early Thirties, but it never applied to school-leavers. Indeed, my problem was in avoiding gainful employment, there was so much of it about.

On every main road in every city in Ireland there were shops of all sizes and descriptions, single-mindedly competing with each other. These shopkeepers didn't wait for the housewives to come to them — they sent their representatives out to knock the housewives' doors. That's if you can call a message boy a representative, because he was the one who did the knocking.

The average message boy's pay for a sixty hour week was six shillings. Fridays and Saturdays were thirteen hour days. We might not have been able to spell exploitation, but we knew what we disliked, so the turnover in the job market was high. The place was coming down with jobs.

Upon leaving school at fourteen I was very happy to be unemployed. Trouble was, there was all that poverty in the house and it made a young fellow feel rotten when he was offered a job and didn't want to take it. Images of the mother at home, with her worry lines, and her hands scarred with the boiling water and caustic soda-based soap, kept appearing in the mind. I once suggested that, for three shillings a week from her housekeeping, I would win Mother the rent money at the horses and render a day job for me unnecessary, but puzzlingly this only made her warm my ear and intensify the job hunt.

Well, one day I walked into our house to find the family in a great state of excitement. Our Tommy, next one up from me on the ladder of seniority in our family by two years, had moved up materially as well. He'd been a message boy in Percy Easton's shop and, because he'd been so good, Percy had spoken for him in a big shop, the Bank Buildings in the centre of Belfast, and wasn't our Tommy going to start work behind the bacon counter at twelve and sixpence a week.

"That's great," I said. "Grand stuff altogether, but why was I fetched in from outside the bookies to learn that? Sure I could have been told it when the racing was over. Excuse me. . . . " I made to leave but I was hauled back into contention.

"You've got Tommy's job in Percy Easton's," Mother said. She looked far too pleased about it for my liking.

"I don't think message boy would suit me," I said.

"Would a welt on the ear suit you any better?" Mother yelled. "You've been nothing but a torment since you left school."

"And another thing," Tommy put in, "don't you be letting me down. I'm leaving that job with a good name."

I took him on on his own terms. "It doesn't take much to have a good name as a message boy," I said. "A chimpanzee could do it. I'd sooner be a bookie's clerk. That's what I call stretching the mind."

But at the age of fourteen a man has no clout. The following Monday morning, as our Tommy excitedly left for his new job working the bacon slicer in the Bank Buildings, I crawled unwillingly to Percy Easton's. I was expecting the worst. I knew my own strong points and describing an arc all around Percy Easton's shop on North Queen Street humping a message boy's basket on my shoulder wasn't one of them. Anyway, from what I had seen of Percy Easton I wasn't all that struck on him. He was a small man, sarcastic to boys and quick to criticize them.

Within the space of the next few weeks it became clear that Percy wasn't exactly dying about me either. When he got smart with me, I got smarter with him.

But being smart only works when you're otherwise free from sin and I wasn't. I mixed up customers' orders, I served a woman with pepper instead of dry ginger and ruined her baking, and as well as that I got on the wrong side of Percy's awful son Ernie, an informer, twelve years of age. Young Ernie saw me pop a chocolate biscuit into my mouth on my very first day.

"I'm gonna tell on you," he said and away he ran two double to squeal to his Da. My head was ringing for half an hour after the wallop that Percy gave me.

Mind you, the job had its compensations; most of the housewives I visited were kind-hearted and good in the line of bread and jam and that kind of thing. One woman called Mrs Cash, who needed the crutches and never left the house and who seemed to have money and lived on her own in a semi-d, poured out her thanks to me when I suggested that she might take up the horses to pass the time away. So I showed her what to do and she turned out to be quite good at them. Each morning I used to collect her bet and leave it into the bookies. She put me on ten per cent of the return and it came as a nice surprise every once in a while when she touched.

I tried to get her to vastly increase her stake, explaining that if my ten per cent could reach an average of six shillings a week I could let on to go to work and spend time at the bookies instead. But when she sat down and worked out what it would take to achieve this on the basis of current performance, it turned out to require an average weekly outlay of about thirty pounds, with probable losses running at twenty seven pounds. So while I was drawing six shilling a week from her, she would be dissipating her fortune at a colossal rate. So that was the end of that theory. Still, at least I brought some interest into one woman's life. Probably the only woman, come to think of it.

Actually, it was a female who was the means of my finally getting out of Percy Easton's. Her name was Isobel Bailey and she lived in Lewisham Street. She was fourteen like me, a pudgy girl with bulges everywhere and eyes with about as much romantic appeal in them as a couple of boiled eggs. She answered the door to me when I called for her mother's grocery order.

"Hey, do you fancy me?" she asked one day.

I was scared out of my wits.

"Fancy you," I blurted out, "is your head cut?"

She glanced back over her shoulder. "Call back when my mother's out," she whispered.

I was so confused that I took her mother's order down all wrong. Mrs Bailey complained to Percy after I made up the goods and delivered them. She carried them into the shop and planted them down on the counter. Isobel was with her.

"He's got nearly everything wrong," Mrs Bailey said.

Percy handed me a whack on the back of the neck, "I'm sorry, Mrs Bailey." He took his pencil from behind his ear and got ready to take her order down.

As he was doing this, Herbie Irons the assistant, the world's worst punter, came in from the bookies three shops down.

"What won that?" I whispered.

"Neapolitan," he whispered back, though he said it as "Napoleon".

"What price?"

"Five to one." My heart leapt. Mrs Cash had a double up. My brain worked rapidly: my ten per cent would run out at five shillings and sixpence. From being a wretch cowed by Isobel Bailey's mother, I grew into a man of confidence and stature.

But Mrs Bailey was speaking. "Ah, but that's not all," she said. "It seems that this young gentleman was wanting to know if he could come into the house with my Isobel when I was out. So what do you think of that now?"

I was leaning on a broom at the time; my mouth fell open

at the lie. Isobel was hanging onto her mother's arm looking down, the picture of innocence.

Percy hit me another wallop and I exploded. Holding my sore ear with the one hand, pointing to Isobel with the other, and resolute in the fire that owning five shillings and sixpence put into the gut, I flung the broom down and yelled, "Take a bloody look at her. Sure, who would want to be on their own with that? She looks about as attractive as a hundredweight of turnips!"

Well, Isobel started to roar and cry, her mother shouted all over the place and Percy Easton sacked me on the spot.

But what did I care? I was a man of means, there was a good thing out at Plumpton the next day and I would be there to have a whale at it. I walked out of Percy Easton's for good.

Awful Ernie was waiting outside to gloat. He was standing exactly halfway between me and the bookies where I was now going to lift Mrs Cash's bet.

"Now you're in trouble," Ernie chanted.

Absently, for I was going over the rest of the next day's card at Plumpton in my mind, I buried the toe of my boot in Ernie's arse, then took a deep, relieved breath. By God, but there were times when a man was glad to be alive.

High Finance

When I was thirteen I backed an article called Squadron Castle for threepence, the other threepence being carried by a mate of mine Billy Henry. It won at a hundred to eight.

This horse later won the Lincoln Handicap on a day when at fifteen I had finally persuaded a dame called Jinny Corbett to come to the pictures with me. Jinny Corbett, also fifteen and well upholstered, was reputed to be red hot at the pictures; she was said to be like the giant anaconda once she got going. The day that the news came through that Squadron Castle won the Lincoln I was standing in the queue waiting to get into the pictures, with Jinny Corbett already starting her antics, holding my hand and standing very close.

"What won the Lincoln?" I asked Tommy Waters, who happened to be passing.

"Squadron Castle," he said glumly. I slapped my brow.

"Hell roast it," I exclaimed. "I didn't notice it as a runner or I'd have backed it. What the hell price was it?"

"A hundred to plenty," Tommy Waters told me and I let rip with more expletives, letting go of Jinny Corbett's hand in order to keep slapping my brow.

By the time my composure had returned Jinny Corbett had vanished. There was no point in going to the pictures therefore, so I went home, wrote a suicide note, went up to Alexandra Park and sat on the damp grass, intending to give myself the cold and sicken and die of it. However, realising after three minutes that it wasn't the greatest way to go, I went and sought out Jinny Corbett.

"Where did you go?" I asked her. She tossed her head.

"I was disgusted by your language," she said. "With you being a boy chorister and in the Church Lads' Brigade I thought I was going to the pictures with somebody who knew nothing about sex. That's where my interests lie. But after listening to that first mouthful to Tommy Waters it was clear that you're steeped in sinful habits. I'm not about to carry on with somebody who knows the game inside out," and she walked away, out of my life, not realising that she'd missed the thrill of thrills, for I knew less than nothing about the game. Up until then I'd regarded girls as soft boys. She would have been the first dame I'd taken even to the pictures, never mind anything else.

But that was all to come. Let us now go back to our opening scene, two years earlier. The time that Billy Henry and I backed Squadron Castle it won at a hundred to eight. By the time we had bought ourselves ten Woodbine and an ice-cream poke each, we had six shillings and a couple of coppers. We were feeling confident.

"Hold on to a shilling between us and stick five shillings onto the second favourite," I said and we got Sammy Doak to carry the bet in.

As luck would have it, the next race was a gentleman jockey's race with about twenty runners and none of them worth a crack. So the betting was very open with the favourite at eleven to two and the second favourite sitting clear at eight to one, and of course you know what's coming – the blasted horse won for us.

Oh, calamity. We now had forty six shillings on our hands!

Billy Henry and I were in a real state of nerves. Sammy Doak nearly collapsed when we tipped him ten shillings just for carrying the bet, but we had to try to get the money down to working class proportions. Sammy took one look at the note and took off for Paddy McEldowney's pub at the foot of the street like a streak of lightning. But we were still left with thirty six shillings on our hands.

"What on earth are we going to do?" Billy Henry wailed.

"Cram it onto a big outsider," I suggested.

"But what the frick are we going to do if it wins?" Billy screamed. He was always using substitute swear words.

I shook my head; the consequences were too dire to contemplate.

We went and knocked doors and invited the half of the lads of the street to McDevitt's shop where we bought them smokes and sweets. And we were still left with one pound ten shillings between us. It was the most we'd ever handled in our lives. We were terrified. We each bought a shilling string of beads for our mothers from a draper's shop in York Street and there we were, still with twenty eight bob left.

"It's just not possible to spend it," Billy said hopelessly.

"I'll tell you what," I said finally. I took a shilling and

41

handed it to Billy and I took another for myself.

"See that twenty six bob," I said, "well I'll go and bury it underneath the nasturtiums in the box in our back yard. We'll take out a shilling a day for racing purposes. That'll keep us in stake money for a calendar month, OK?"

He nodded, but he was every bit as uneasy as I was. A guaranteed sixpenny double every racing day for a month brought a funny feeling with it, a feeling of deprivation strangely enough. I hadn't realised until then how much better fun it was to be broke, rising to the challenge of generating bet money from nothing.

"It's funny," I said in a hushed voice, "great wealth brings its own worries, doesn't it?"

"I don't know about that," Billy Henry said, "but it'll fricking bring me a thick ear if my old woman finds out about it."

I took the dough home and buried it underneath the nasturtiums, then I went into the kitchen. Mother was sitting at the table with my sister Charlotte and the two of them were cutting the tripe out of another woman in the street for having the electric light installed in her lavatory out in the back yard.

"My God," Mother was saying, "what in heaven's name would you want electric light in there for? It's not as if it's a hard place to find anything in." Then she looked up at me. I threw the beads onto the table.

"Bought you those," I said.

"Och, do you know, they're just lovely son," Mother took them in her hand and studied them.

"Got them in a wee shop on the New Lodge Road for a penny," I said, "and I just thought they would do you for something like the Mothers' Union outing to Garron Tower."

"They're beautiful. And a nice shade of green," Mother said and it was nine to four on that I was getting a kiss, but just with that Charlotte's eyes narrowed; she lifted the beads and studied them.

"I've seen those beads in Greenaway's the drapers," she said. "You gave far more than a penny for them."

Now our Charlotte and I weren't exactly on the best of terms because I'd called "Hello Fatso!" to her in the Lyceum picture house a couple of nights earlier. She wasn't fat, in fact she was very nice, but I had found that calling her fat sent her nearly round the twist. And in the Lyceum that time she was with some fellow, so one way and another she had it in for me.

"Where did you get the money for these?" she was demanding when the door was suddenly pushed open and in walked Mrs Henry, mother of Billy. She was pushing Billy in front of her and a string of beads were hanging from her fingers like the rosary thingamies, only of course we didn't have rosaries – quite the opposite.

"Good afternoon Mrs McAughtry," she said to Mother.

"Good afternoon Mrs Henry," said Mother.

With the formalities over Mrs Henry, who was a well-built woman, bent over the table to me, tightening her grip on Billy's shoulder, making him scrunch himself up like the hunchback of Notre Dame.

"He says you gave him them," she said, showing me the beads.

At that time we were doing analysis and parsing at school

43

and for some reason, in this moment of peril, my mind jumped from the danger to the study of language. "How would you analyse that?" I asked myself. "He says" the principal clause; "you gave him them" a subordinate clause. But what kind? Was it adverbial? It certainly followed upon the verb "to say".

"Is it all right if I hit him, Mrs McAughtry?" Mrs Henry asked Mother.

"Go ahead, Mrs Henry," Mother nodded graciously. Whereupon Mrs Henry put a knuckle into my cheek and turned it round and round, boring it in.

"He says you gave him them," she repeated.

"Maybe it's actually two principal clauses," I thought, but the knuckle was nearly through to the teeth.

I let go of English and took a look at Billy Henry. He was a wreck: both sides of his mouth had been knuckle-bored and his nerves were gone.

I shrugged, "We made a stack of money at the horses. It's out there, buried under the nasturtiums."

In two blurs the women left for the back yard; they even seemed to get there by going through the closed door. Then back they came, with Mother holding the twenty six shillings and her fingers all mould.

"Where did you say you got this?" the two women demanded. Wearily I named the horses, the meeting, distances, weights carried, jockeys on board and the odds to each winner. They were satisfied. They split the money between them and Mrs Henry, shoving Billy in front of her, left.

"Now I'm putting you up the stairs to stay there, for you've my heart broke," Mother said. And that's what she did. And she never even thanked me for the beads.

Seeing the Light

*I*t was the early Thirties and the whole of Belfast had for
months been convulsed by a fit of religion. So strong was
the spiritual voltage that the Protestant population ran out
of churches and holy places and there was a huge overspill
of penitent sinners running mission services without benefit
of clergy in ordinary kitchen and parlour houses. The whole
city was hymn-happy, no doubt about it. It's a good thing
there was no speed or ecstasy or crack or any other class of
a hallucinatory drug about in those days or that's what it
would have been blamed on, as round as a hoop.

All up and down the street folk were calling each other
Brother and Sister and flashing smiles in all directions. Before
I was converted myself, I tried to cash in on the prevailing
mood by going into Martha McDevitt's wee shop and saying, "Good morning Sister," because I had noticed Martha
coming out of one of the meetings. Martha didn't reply. She
just did what she always did and stared at me suspiciously.

"What is it you want?" she enquired.

"Praise the Lord and all His works," I said for openers, "and
I was wondering, Sister, whether you could let me have five
Woodbine on strap."

For reply Martha McDevitt hauled off and belted me one across the side of the gub. That's when I came to realise that religion is one thing, but commerce is another and there's no connection between the two.

I had gone up to the mission hall at the top of Collyer Street out of feelings that were the very opposite of Christian, let it be said. For I had been told by Davy McCarthy that Butler Forsythe had seen the light and that he was going to give his testimony that very night.

"What's a testimony?" I wanted to know.

"I'm not sure," said Davy, "but according to what I've heard it means spilling the beans, good and proper."

I looked at Davy McCarthy, horror pictured all across my face.

"Knocking off the caramels out of Fee's shop, that kind of thing," Davy added and we both sucked in our breath.

Well, Davy, Frankie Pattison and I turned up at the mission hall. Through the problem being a religious one, none of us said anything to Butler beforehand about his intentions. But, after about half an hour of praying and hand-clapping and hallelujahs, we found out.

"Them'ns what feel the need to give their testimony, get fell in facing me," said Norman Quinn the preacher, who had been twenty two years in the Ulster Rifles and had a hook for a hand, through hanging onto a grenade too long because he was slow counting to ten.

The sinners spoke up, not that any of them were all that interesting. Since they were grown-ups, we were entitled to expect the kind of stories we'd heard from the men at our street corner, stories of pub fights or maybe knocking off bottles of stout out of the bottling store in the yard at McGranaghan's pub while letting on to relieve themselves, that kind of thing – but no.

These grown-ups giving their testimony weren't in the same class as the men from our street. Dear knows where Norman Quinn had dug them up. Most of the guilt of these ones seemed to concern sinful thoughts and any one of us in our gang could have left them standing in that department. I would have had more sinful thoughts before my breakfast than this lot had had in their whole lives. Some of the things that I had wished on jockeys and trainers would have set the mission hall on fire if I'd mentioned them.

But in due course up stood Butler and we held our breath.

"I was a backslider!" Butler began.

"Well, so what," we thought: all the other repentant sinners were backsliders too.

"I knocked off caramels out of Fee's sweet shop," Butler shouted. "When you ask for gub stoppers, she has to turn round and get them from a high shelf and you can KO a caramel from beside the scales if you're quick."

The balloon was going up. Clearly something had to be done. Davy McCarthy did it.

"Good for you for owning up!" he shouted. "Thank the Lord no other boys committed that sin, did they Butler?"

"Yeah, did they Butler?" the rest of us asked.

Butler stood thinking, then he said, "They did, but I'm not for telling on them."

"Hallelujah!" we all shouted.

48

"Praise the Lord," said the preacher and that was more or less that.

"Mind you," said Butler to the rest of us on the way home, "I wasn't going to clash on you regarding knocking off the caramels. After all, I took the oath of the Four Tea Leaves never to clash on any member of the gang."

That was the name of our gang at that time, the Four Tea Leaves. We took the name after a teacher in school had told us the story of Ali Baba and the Forty Thieves. Butler Forsythe at the time was suffering from waxy ear and he only half-heard the teacher. "Hey, that was a brilliant story, about Ali Baba and the Four Tea Leaves," he said, so that's the name that we adopted.

"The punishment for clashing," Frankie Pattison reminded him, "is being tied to the ground, covered with honey and eaten alive by ants." We dandered home, more or less satisfied with the way a crisis had been overcome.

On the way, I fell in step with Butler. "Tell me this, how do you get to be saved?" I asked.

"You'll soon know if it happens to you," he said. "It makes you, like, walk on air and you feel like singing hymns all the time."

"What's a backslider?" I wanted to know next.

"Hell roast me if I could tell you," he replied, "but that's what you're supposed to say when you're giving your testimony."

I was thinking. "Do you know this," I said, "you mightn't believe it, but I have got a kind of a feeling like as if I'm walking on air too." I began to hum *Shall We Gather At The River*.

"That's definitely it," Butler said. "You're converted."

"Hallelujah!" I shouted.

Reaching home, I put my head around our kitchen door. It was cold in there because Mother had the yard door open hanging up the washing. The wind was whistling through the house and the family were all huddled round the fire, which itself was burning low. It would have been very foolish for any of the family to go and get a shovel of coal for it because there would be no way of getting your seat back, so there they were, the family, the whole five of them, clinging to their places, like pups on the bitch's tits.

"I'm converted," I announced from the door. "I'm saved. Hallelujah."

"Oh good," our Jim said, "well then you can go and get a shovel of coal for the fire."

"What? And me not even sitting at it?" I retorted. "Away and catch yourself on."

"Getting a shovel of coal is exactly the sort of thing that saved people are supposed to do," Jack said. With a sniff I went and got the shovel of coal and hurled it past the lot of them onto the fire. Then I pushed my way as close as I could to the heat and began to sing *Be Thou My Vision O Lord Of My Heart*.

Next morning was Saturday. I was sitting studying the racing page of the *Northern Whig* and humming the Twenty Third Psalm when Mother came out of the scullery.

"Take this physic before your breakfast son," she said. In one of her hands was the bottle of castor oil and in the other was a spoon.

50

This was the regular Saturday morning ritual in just about every kitchen house in the city of Belfast. For some mothers it was syrup of figs for the physic, others went for senna pods, while the kids whose luck was really out had to swallow the vile-tasting Epsom salts. But castor oil wasn't exactly golden syrup either. I hated it.

"I'm fed up taking that oul stuff," I protested.

Mother held up a finger. "Saved people always take their physic," she said, so I screwed up my face and managed to get the stuff down, hurrying up to swallow bread and butter and sugar after it for castor oil had a desperate lingering taste and smell.

Next thing it was a matter of who was going to get the bacon ends for the Saturday fry at tea-time. Wisely, the rest of the family had disappeared.

"Love, would you go down to the pork store and get the bacon ends for me?" Mother asked.

"How many kids are in this house?" I wanted to know, "I went to the pork store last week. It's somebody else's turn. What am I, some kind of a dumb slave?"

Mother shook her head sadly. "Honour thy father and thy mother, that thy days may be long in the land," she said.

In the street I met Butler Forsythe.

"Coming down to the pork store with me?" I asked. He nodded.

"Be as well to hurry up," he said, "I've just had my syrup of figs."

"I know," I said, "castor oil, me. But I think we can make it."

All the way to the pork store Butler was quiet. Then he said, "Do you know this, I'm fed up of being saved."

"Right enough I noticed that you weren't humming the hymns," I remarked.

Butler went on, "ever since I've seen the light I've done nothing but run the messages and get shovels of coal for the fire."

"Me similar," I said, "what do you think?"

We stood for a good while, thinking, until the physic started to hit me.

"Have to go," I said.

"Me too," Butler said looking uneasy.

"Tell you what," I said, "after this we'll go up the park and throw clods at the kids from North Queen Street. What about that?"

Butler nodded. "OK," he said, turning to run. "Sure we can always get converted again tomorrow."

The Ingersoll Watch

*I*n the early Thirties, when I was fourteen and out of work as usual, my brother Mart was paid off from McCue Dick's, the timber yard down alongside the docks. He had been working there as a labourer carrying what he and his workmates called "dales" – long, heavy loads of timber. The nearest I can get to a derivation of the word is that it is the Belfast way of saying deal, meaning fir or pine wood. The shoulders of his working jacket were ripped and torn to the lining and he often had to have skelfs, or wood splinters, picked out of his hands. Mart would have been twenty then.

Father's ship came in shortly afterwards and it was arranged that Mart would go away with Dad on the s.s. Dunaff Head. He signed on as a trimmer. He would be working in the gloomy coal bunker, wheeling barrowloads of coal to a chute and emptying it down to the stokehold, where two firemen fed it to the fires that heated the water that made the steam that drove the engines that powered the ship that took our Mart away from me. It was a dreadful job. Mother hated the sea and it broke her heart to see Mart go, but there was nothing else at the time. I missed him terribly too, but I kept it to myself.

The day he went away on his first trip I left him down to the ship, carrying his "donkey's breakfast" – the straw-filled mattress that each sailor had to supply for himself. I watched as he stowed his bits and pieces. His bunk was fastened to steel plates that simply wept condensation. There was no need for the sea to get in: he was going to sleep under wet blankets anyway, like a real seadog.

Mart was on the twelve to four watch. At half past eleven in the morning he had to be shown the routine, so he climbed into his new dungarees and stiff heavy boots, wrapped a fresh length of rag around his neck, put on an old cap and he was ready to start. I went with him to the bunker hatch.

"I never even had time to study the horses," he said, "so I can't tip you one, but have this on something for yourself." He gave me a shilling. For the first time in my life I shook hands formally with him. Then he went down the shining steel steps and was lost to me.

I walked down the gang-plank, went through the dock gates, up Whitla Street, up Duncairn Gardens and round to our house.

"Did he get fixed up all right?" Mother asked.

"He did," I said.

I took my jacket off, hung it over the banister and went upstairs to the back attic where I slept. Some previous tenant had tried to make a bathroom out of our back attic, but the project was doomed because the water wouldn't carry that high, so we just bathed in the scullery with the curtain pulled. On the day that Mart went away I lay on the camp bed beside the useless bath and cried my eyes out.

Later, when I was more at myself, I studied the card at Kempton and spotted a horse called Adieu. The hint was so obvious that I didn't even look at its form. I shoved Mart's shilling on its nose and waited confidently for it to win.

The bloody thing was beaten out of sight. I doubt if he was ever seen again. The ghost of Adieu is probably running in the long grass by the back straight at Kempton Park and I'll bet an even fiver he's still at the back of a ghostly field.

This experience taught me one very valuable lesson – in a normal racecard never, never back a horse unless there are form reasons for doing so. After the death sentence was pronounced on that shilling, I looked up the form of Adieu. It couldn't have beaten my granny. Sentiment and punting don't mix. If I were nowadays to see a horse that bore my dead mother's full name and last known address, I wouldn't back it with Russian roubles.

From then on, as Mart settled into his new life, I wrote both to Dad and to Mart. We had always had to write to Dad once every voyage. The rest of the family found it a chore. Mother would suggest items of news for each of the family, but still their letters only ran to three-quarters of a page of big, big writing. Our Jim thought up a good wheeze though. His letters suddenly took up the whole page. Here's how they went:

"Dear Daddy, Just a few lines hoping to find you well, as this leaves us all well at home. Well Daddy, we are learning new sums at school. Here's one: . . . " and he would space out a good long addition sum down the page, stick in the answer and end it with "Your loving son Jim."

For me, however, writing was never a problem. I could rattle off a letter to Dad full of general news and then write maybe half a dozen pages to Mart, updating him on the horsey stuff. Once I told him a sad tale:

"I fancied a novice chaser called Red Socks going in the two o'clock at Haydock, but I sat outside the bookies acting the goat with Bobby McCandless and didn't notice the time passing. By the time I sent my sixpence in for Red Socks it was a minute past the time for the off and you know old Rafferty the bookie, he wouldn't hear tell of a bet even a second after the off, in case one of us might be a wireless operator in touch with the course. And wouldn't you know it, Red Socks came in at six to one."

I went on: ". . . My mate Tommy Watson was there. He, of course, has a wrist watch. Nobody's allowed to forget it. 'If you'd only asked me the time by my new watch that wouldn't have happened,' he said, shoving his watch under my nose. I felt like crashing my fist into his face . . ."

A month later I came into the house from keeping Bobby McCandless company walking his greyhounds. I sat up to the table for my tea and I wondered why all the family were smiling and looking mysterious. Then I spotted it: by the side of my plate was a slim package addressed to me, the stamps were Canadian and the writing was our Mart's.

"Dear Sam,

This will help you to get your bet on before the off from now on. It will also save Tommy Watson from having his face crashed in . . . "

It was an Ingersoll sports watch. No present that I have ever received since that day so long ago has ever given me so much pleasure. It was beautiful, a white face with golden hands and a real leather strap. When I put it on I was a totally different person.

"Where'd you get your watch?" I asked Tommy Watson.

"From Chapman's shop, up at the corner of Collyer Street," he said shooting out his cuff, the way he'd been doing for weeks.

"This one came from Montreal, in Canada," I said, easing the sleeve back and holding mine under his nose. "It's an Ingersoll sports, as used by the Mounties."

Oh, but I had a lovely time with that watch. It changed my whole personality. It was impossible to insult me. To every jibe I gave a cherubic smile; provocation met gracious and understanding nods. I was enjoying myself. I was giving Tommy Watson the complete ab dabs, driving him at one point to say, "There's a shop down the town that's stuffed with Ingersolls."

"But is it stuffed with Canadian ones?" I replied. "Is it stuffed with watches tested to work at forty below, eh?"

Then, when I'd only had the watch for two weeks – disaster. I went to the last house of the pictures with Tommy Watson, came out after the show, walked back to the street corner, struck up a yarn with the boys, went to look at my watch – and it was gone.

The strap must have been wrongly fastened; it had fallen off. Tommy Watson and I set off back, searching for it on the pavement all the way. The manager of the picture house allowed us to search the place where we'd sat; he even gave us his torch, although the lights were on. But no luck. My magnificent Ingersoll watch was lost.

Worse, Mart was due home in exactly one week. What on earth was I to tell him?

My brain went to work. "Where's the shop that's stuffed with Ingersolls?" I asked Tommy Watson. He took me there at once. My heart sank: they were twelve and sixpence each.

Next morning I was there when the shop opened. I went in and told the whole sad tale to the manager.

"What's the very cheapest you could let me have it?" I pleaded. He thought for a minute.

"Twelve shillings and sixpence," he said.

"Watch that soft heart of yours," I told him, "it'll be the death of you one day."

I went down to the Midland railway station on York Street and carried bags for passengers. This was dangerous work. It was the preserve of a Shore Road gang, about twenty strong. When I'd earned a shilling, one twentieth of the gang caught me at it and loosened one of my teeth. But I took the shilling to an all day pitch and toss school that was running in the old kilns where the brick factory used to be on the Limestone Road. There I waited until a run started. Billy Bates, who did clerking for a bookie at the dogs, headed the coins three times in a row; I took him to make it four and I was right. That was two shillings.

It's never good sense to stay at the pitch and toss if you get the first bet up, so I went racing at Pontefract but I had to take no chances. The going was heavy, the prize money was buttons and there was only one half-decent class race on the card — a two mile 'chase. I stuck the two shillings on the good thing at two to one on. It obliged and that was three shillings.

That night Tommy Watson shook me by handing me two shillings. I was so taken aback by his generosity that I got my thank you speech all mixed up. "Don't think I won't forget this," I said, "because I will."

Next day was a Sunday. On the Monday I had a shilling on a loser. It shook me. I was frozen; I did no more bets. So the kitty was down to four shillings again.

The day after, I was sitting watching a pontoon school at the street corner. Big Leachy, home from the States, drew a six, then a five. He dug his hand into his pocket and pulled out a handful of silver. I took two of my shillings out and threw them down beside Big Leachy's bet. He drew a face card and the bank paid only twenty. That was six shillings. Mart was due home in three days.

Racing was abandoned that day due to flooding. The day after I went down to the railway again and managed one and sixpence from bag carrying before a scout for the Shore Road gang appeared on the horizon. I scooted off at a rate of knots. Now it was seven and six.

"Where's your watch, Sam?" Mother asked that evening. I told her it was with a man in Canning Street who could regulate watches.

"It was losing a minute a day," I said. "I suppose it's the unaccustomed heat of these latitudes. He has to keep it for three days to work out the exact loss."

Next day, in the first race, I lost the one and six on a hurdler called Upside Down. That's just the way he finished, upside down at the last hurdle, leading from here to Carrickfergus. I was unnerved. Then I saw Tommy Watson coming up the street.

"I couldn't stick the suspense," he said, "I sneaked out of the shipyard. How are you going?" I told him — six shillings.

"What are you going to do?" he asked. I shook my head resignedly.

"It's too late now for caution," I said. He handed me a shilling.

"That's the tank," he said.

Things were too fraught for me even to thank him. I took the shilling and studied the card. There was a novice chaser with a good second under its belt. It was sitting at five to four in the paper betting. It's name was Xerxes. Knowing the reading standard of the punters round our way I was unwilling to trust any of them to pronounce Xerxes, so I wrote the name down and handed it to the next man going into the bookies.

"Have that seven shillings on that horse," I said and my voice was so husky that it almost broke. He came out a minute later and handed me my docket.

"I fancy that one myself," he said. "Its about due a win, that Exercise."

Then I walked away and stood by the corner. Tommy Watson understood: he left me alone. I stood like a graven image until the result was bound to be in. Then I went back. "What won that one?" I asked the punters who were streaming out. . . .

". . . How's the watch going?" Mart asked next day, as I waited for him to scrub himself down and get dressed to go ashore.

My hand rocketed out from under my cuff.

"It's just about brilliant," I said. "I'm expecting a call from Greenwich Observatory, to see if their clock's OK."

"So it stood up to the journey, did it?"

"Stood up?" I said. "For dear sake, you would think it never was on a journey."

Play Up and Play the Game

*A*way back in the mid-Thirties, Belfast Corporation laid down a pitch and putt course in the Grove playing fields where they ran alongside the Shore Road in North Belfast. Soon after it opened, we were into golf at a mile a minute.

We knew and loved this area anyway. When I was a message boy working for Percy Easton, I used to meet other message boys there, halfway through the morning, behind a hoarding where a hollow lay. It all started with an arrangement between myself and Sanno Whelan, who delivered messages for a butcher on North Queen Street. We would meet behind the hoarding, swap gossip and eat broken biscuits.

In general, grocers tended to look the other way when message boys took the odd handful of broken biscuits as a perk. In normal handling, biscuits broke: all that I did was increase the breakage. I could live with it. Sanno Whelan's contribution was the odd Woodbine that he got for fetching cheap wine from the Gibraltar Bar to an old lady in Spencer Street.

In time, other boys joined us, until on a good morning there would be maybe seven or eight baskets full of goods lying on the grass behind the hoardings and seven or eight message boys comparing notes, eating broken biscuits and passing Woodbines from one to the other. Not all the lads worked for grocers — one delivered for a poultryman and one was a chemist's boy.

When the pitch and putt course was laid down, naturally none of us knew anything about the game, but the idea wasn't hard to grasp. We left our baskets in view, scraped up the tuppence for the hire of one set of clubs — an iron and a putter — tossed for who was to play and away we went around the course.

At first it was just a novelty, good clean fun, as everybody else treated the game. But it wouldn't be Tiger's Bay if the gambling didn't come into it and, sure enough, in a couple of weeks the bets were going down.

It started with broken biscuits, laying odds hole by hole. But the broken ones were mostly digestives and you can go off digestive biscuits after a while. And anyway, the grocers were beginning to ask questions as to how the stiffening seemed to have gone out of their biscuits, all of a sudden. In those days grocers were allowed to hit message boys and lots of them did, certainly Percy Easton thumped me a good few times, and there's only so many blows a lad can take to the head, before the head tells the hands to go a bit easier when they're handling the biscuits. That's when Sanno Whelan saw the chance to make a contribution. We began to bet in sausages as well, these being money for jam for Sanno to knock off out of the butchers.

I was rather good at the pitch and putt.

"Where are you getting all the sausages?" Mother asked.

"There's a flaw in them," I told her. "They're either too fat or too thin and this butcher's very fussy about that, so he gives them to Sanno Whelan his message boy, and he gives them to me."

Times were hard so she didn't pursue the matter, but every now and again I would catch Mother giving me the narrow eye as if to say you're getting away with it this time, but when the economy recovers you're a candidate for a thick ear.

A golfer watching us on what we liked to call the links would have been puzzled to splindereens. For a start, only two were playing but each player had a minder. The minute the ball was struck the striker would take to his heels and run like the clappers after it, and as he flew over the course so a mate of his opponent would run alongside him to where the ball lay.

Now the average golfer would regard this as strange behaviour indeed. The usual routine is to drive off, watch the flight of the ball, shake the head, look pensive, try the stroke again with no ball there any more and then stand back while the opponent does the same. But there was nothing average about us. There wasn't one of us that trusted the other to leave the ball where it landed. We simply weren't made that way.

Our intention in playing pitch and putt wasn't to get the sun, or to kill an idle hour, nor was it to try to overcome the challenge that the course presented. No – our intention was to win broken biscuits or sausages. If a nudge with the foot against the ball helped towards that end, well then, the ball was in for a nudging.

So, for the number of holes that the game lasted, what the watcher would have seen would have been a game that burned up more energy than ice hockey. If the ball were to land out of sight, like in a bit of a dip, then the players and the minders were nothing but a blur. And since even this tight supervision didn't always save the ball from a kicking, it wasn't uncommon to see a fist fight breaking out, particularly at the dog-leg fourth. With us, golf was a contact game.

The simple truth of the matter was that there were no sportsmen, as the term is generally understood, amongst us. Certainly the churches tried to argue for fair play, but we just regarded that as yet another near-impossible condition for getting into heaven. We didn't breed good losers. There was no such thing in our book as giving the sucker an even break. Sport, all up and down North Belfast, was run along the same lines as the Massacre at Glencoe.

But we looked after our own, mind. That's why we message boys rallied round when Sanno Whelan was nailed knocking off the sausages, got the sack from his butcher boss, went to join the army as a bugler boy and got turned down because he was too light. Right enough, he looked it. His hips were like two peas in a hanky, he was only five feet and he couldn't have weighed more than six stone. He didn't even do any running at the golf, just watched while the rest of us did.

The army doctor told him to come back when he'd put another half a stone on.

"Funny thing," I said to him, when he came down behind the hoarding to break the news, "you must have carted a mile of sausages here to us for weeks and you weren't eating the things yourself."

"I hate them," he explained, "I hate all meat, after working in the butchers."

He didn't need to go any further. Each one of us hated something. I hated turnips, carrots and parsnips myself. In the house I used to slide them off the plate into my left hand, finish the rest of the dinner, then go upstairs and throw them up the chimney in our front bedroom where the fire was never lit except in time of sickness. To this very day, when I see a waitress or waiter carrying carrots, parsnips or turnips, I feel like scooping them up in my left hand and throwing them up the nearest chimney.

I got Sanno to promise to come down behind the hoarding every working day to keep in touch and he said yes, but he went away very quiet, and the rest of us sat discussing his plight. His father was dead, gassed at the Somme – only lasted five years after the First War. There were brothers and sisters and we could see where he was going to have a problem putting the weight on. We talked about it, remembering that Sanno was quiet, that he felt bad about not being strong enough to run at the golf, that he had given us the only thing he could – his boss's sausages – and we worked out a plan.

Next morning we met as usual, hired out the clubs and started the game. "You've to be my minder," I said to Sanno and my opponent and I took fine care not to run too hard, so that Sanno could keep up. After the time was up, we picked up our baskets and got ready to go.

"Here," I said, handing Sanno half a pound of butter and a packet of good creamy biscuits.

"And take that as well," somebody else said, handing him two soda farls out of a baker's shop.

"And d'ye see these tablets, they're for iron in your blood," said the chemist's boy.

"That's what you call a boiling fowl," the lad from the poultry shop said.

Sanno staggered away under the weight of it all.

"And don't forget to come here tomorrow," we all shouted.

For the next month we carried out the greatest mass knocking-off in history. We knew that we were feeding Sanno's whole family, but there was nothing else for it. They were lean times and his mother was like mine had been with the sausages – she was deferring the enquiry until after the hunger died.

Every day we got Sanno to exercise, running at the golf to watch that there was no skullduggery, or at least that's what he thought he was doing. He got cod liver oil, fresh eggs, the best of good butter, soda and potato farls, boiling fowl and even bars of Cadbury chocolate.

It took a month of knocking-off, but we did it. One day Sanno came to us with a big smile on his face. It was still a farthing face, but he was weighing in at six stone eight and he was going for a boy soldier. And they say that crime doesn't pay.

The Burlington

Uncle James, one of my mother's brothers, stayed single for longer than the average man. He didn't actually get married until he was well into his forties. Anyway, he'd have been a mug to get married before he did, because he certainly had a smashing time single.

Uncle James was black-haired and this was considered lucky. Just after midnight every New Year's morning he would arrive at the door to first-foot our house, having just first-footed Aunt Berry his sister, with whom he lived in Mackey Street. Each New Year he would arrive with a different woman, every one a stormer and every one of them delighted to be in his company. He would bring whisky and wine and carry a piece of coal for luck, and one of my earliest recollections as a child was of waking up to the sound of loud laughing and talking and the clinking of glasses as the New Year toasts were drunk. In the wee room off the kitchen, where I slept with our Jim, that was my cue to fall out of bed – accidentally – so that Mother would come in and gather me up and bring me into the kitchen, to the warm atmosphere of love and goodwill, the yellow gaslight, the laughter and the lovely smell of drink.

Mother and her sisters were quite proud of Uncle James's drawing power with the women. The subject was brought up most often by Aunt Berry, but that's because she was unmarried, having lost her leg just into her teens after a blister on her heel went out of control. Aunt Berry, who was good-looking herself, was a wild romantic.

Uncle James lived a life that was full of incident, although in anybody else's life most of the incidents wouldn't have been worth the mention. It was he way he told them. He had been a soldier in the artillery during the First War and he'd once been kicked on the head by a horse in France. Privately, this was regarded by the family as the reason why he was so excitable. But if that was so, the horse did him a good turn because, as I grew older, I came to love his lively nature and exaggerated actions and reactions, the way his eyes would come alive, the way his face became a part of the story, as the words tore out of him like conversation lozenges out of a machine gun.

He worked for a while in Sandes Soldiers' Home, one of an Empire-wide string of shops where serving soldiers relaxed over tea and buns. Uncle James worked in the one opposite Victoria Barracks on Clifton Street in Belfast. But he got the mallet out of that job when the manager, in remonstrating with him, made the mistake of giving him a push. Three seconds later the customers were sending for cold water for the back of your man's neck, to stop the nosebleed. Another job, navvying in England, came to an end when the ganger, a Cockney, called Uncle James a bone-lazy Belfast git. Before he could take the description a word further, the ganger found himself looking up at the world from the bottom of a drainage trench.

He ended his working days on the buses, but the job he enjoyed best of all was when his brother my Uncle Hugh, in partnership with another man, opened up a small bookie's pitch around the Markets part of Belfast and Uncle James was the payout clerk or, as they call it nowadays, the settler. Right enough he had a lightning fast brain where arithmetic was concerned. This would have been in the early Thirties, when I was no goat's toe as a boy punter in my own right.

The early days of the pitch were exciting times. Uncle James and Aunt Berry kept my mother in close touch with the swings and roundabouts of the racing game and I was a very attentive listener. Mother, bless her, knew nothing about the subject and when we were alone she would sometimes ask me to explain, in simple terms, the import of the good or bad news she'd just heard.

Bookmakers in those days were all unlicensed and were liable at any time to be raided by the police and fined. The timing of such raids was entirely random, at the whim of the local head constable.

"They took us to court again," Uncle James would say. "Five pounds fine. It took away every halfpenny of profit. We worked the long day for nothing."

Another time: "At the last race the pitch looked like winning twenty five quid on the day, when in walked a stranger, well-dressed, looked like a solicitor or something, stuck ten quid on the favourite, it won at five to two, he lifted it, walked out and there we were, wrecked."

"That's lost money too, Lizzie," he would go on. "With the locals we're sure to get it back sooner or later, but we'll not see Lord Muck again, that's a fact."

It was funny to see my church-going Christian mother standing shaking her head at the news, like any punter hearing his bet was down the sluice.

Mind you, these hard cheese stories didn't seem to reflect the true state of things for the business. It was just that Uncle James was fonder of telling hard luck tales, they gave him more scope for wringing out his emotions than the other sort. In fact, the job in the bookies marked the start of some of the hardest boozing and most sustained partying ever seen from him.

"James was late home again last night, Lizzie," Aunt Berry would report. "No sign of him when I went to bed at twelve and he was snoring, with his clothes all over the kitchen, when I got up this morning."

Uncle James had chummed up with the partner in the pitch, a man called Sean. This was a good-looking man, described by Aunt Berry as gorgeous, with dark curly hair ". . . and the loveliest teeth, Lizzie. God, you want to see them, they're like an advert." Aunt Berry was susceptible to men's looks much more than her sisters. Not surprising, with her handicap.

But mind you, somebody else was watching this exciting story unfold as well. A cousin of mine wee Hughie, at eleven the same age as myself, lived at the foot of Osborne Street, handy to Uncle James and he was regularly in and out of the house a good bit, asking if anybody wanted any messages

71

run or the like of that, for the backhanders were good in the bookie days. Hughie was reckless. Rules didn't mean much to him. He was inclined to mitch school and to wander far enough and long enough to have had the whole neighbourhood up looking for him.

Well, Uncle James landed home in the early hours one morning, rightly loaded, dropped his trousers and his shoes and socks down in the kitchen and made his way up to bed, where he flaked out at once. Wee Hughie opened the door at about eight in the morning, for he was like the pigeons, an early riser, looking for what was lying about. And what did he spot but Uncle James's trousers, lying in a heap on the ground. He picked them up, went through them, pulled out fifteen pounds plus silver and copper and took off with the lot in a fit of excitement. On the way he met a mate of his Hector Scallion, whose real name was Scanlon, showed Hector the money and the two of them hit the trail for the fleshpots.

The storm broke when Uncle James came downstairs at noon, noticed his trousers had been disturbed and discovered the crime. He and Aunt Berry tried to work things out.

The front door had the key in it and it could have been anybody in the street, but never mind the bad times that they were having, nobody in the street would have done that. Along with Aunt Berry, Uncle James sat, trying in vain to hold his aching head and use it at the same time.

In the event it was Aunt Berry who hit the bullseye.

"There's one character whose name's written all over this," she said. "Wee Hughie. Find him and you'll find the money."

That's when I got to hear the details, because I had just arrived home from school for my lunch and I was sitting at the table with my brothers and sister when the feathers started to fly. A line of relations arrived at the house headed by Uncle James, then came wee Hughie's father and mother, Uncle Alec and Aunt Lena, with Aunt Berry bringing up the rear.

An all-points bulletin had gone out and it was established that wee Hughie wasn't at school. And he'd been seen running down Mackey Street at just after eight that morning.

The spit was forming at the corners of Uncle James's mouth when he arrived. "When I get hold of that wee gangster I'll kick him up the Limestone Road to Dunmore Park and I'll feed him to the bloody greyhounds," he said.

Hughie's father Alec was beside Uncle James listening to this, but he knew the form. He didn't get annoyed. It was the lines and the performance that mattered to Uncle James. The intention expressed was just flim flam: all he wanted was his money back. Uncle Alec just gave a resigned kind of a smile.

Uncle James remembered exactly the amount of money in his pocket when he went to bed. It was fifteen pounds twelve shillings and eight pence, he said. The previous evening his mathematical brain must have been subtracting the price of each round, calculating what was left, even though he was getting drunker and drunker as the evening wore on.

The whole platoon of them sat in our house, drumming their fingers, unable to find a starting point. My brothers and my sister were even sitting frowning, drumming their own fingers, caught up in the general mood. They simply hadn't any idea of where Hughie was, but I had.

"I'll bet you I could find him" I said.

Hope flared.

"Where is he?" Uncle James's voice broke with emotion as he said it. "Take me to him and I'll tie him to the back of a tram and have him trailed back up the Duncairn Gardens. What's left of him I'll throw into the waterworks."

"If he spots any of you you'll never see him till the money's spent," I said, although how on earth anybody alive could spend the twelve shillings and eightpence, never mind the fifteen pounds beat me all ends up.

"Go, son, and find him. And tell him to come home and we'll not bate him," Aunt Lena said, using the standard formula for the times.

If I'd been wee Hughie I wouldn't have had money on the promise, but never mind that: I was off school for the rest of the day and I knew where wee Hughie was. I left the house feeling like the guy in the picture who volunteers to go out into the storm and bring back the snakebite serum. I was heading for the Burlington.

Along York Street, near to the Co-Op store, there was a place known to every man, woman and child of the district. Simply put, it was not possible to walk past and ignore it. In opening hours there was always a little knot of people standing on the pavement, staring into the window. As they stood, they licked their lips, they swallowed, their eyes glazed.

They were looking at the best of hot food: brown chops,

the fatty fringes beautifully frizzled at the edges; sausages sitting row on row, fried and ready to burst at the first incisor tooth contact; bacon crying out to be lifted without benefit of fork between thumb and forefinger, bitten and ripped away from its rind; round, fat, deep brown quoits of mince steak, cooked all the way through; sliced potatoes, fried to a gorgeous yellow-brown finish, sitting in sweet disorder like scattered petals over braised steak; fat green peas, begging to be squashed between knife blade and potato and, at the heart and centre of the display in a huge container, about three gallons of thick, brown, bubbling, nourishing stew.

This was the Burlington.

To the well-waged it was somewhere to fill up, but to the workless adults and all the kids of Tiger's Bay it wasn't a caff: it was a cathedral of gastronomy. It was our ambition one day to take holy communion there. It was odds on that wee Hughie had already knelt at the altar.

I stood looking through the window. Of all the gorgeous dishes on display, as usual the chops were the ones that got to me. In all my life I had never eaten a chop, the whole chop, and nothing but the chop. I had been given the occasional segment from the top left or the bottom right or whatever of our Jack's chop, he being a wage earner on the buses, but I had still to experience the almost indescribable pleasure of holding a hot crackling chop in my two hands and rending and tearing the meat from the bare bone. As I walked into the Burlington I was growling like a young bear at the thought of it. A broad-chested, hairy man was ladling soup into a plate.

"Excuse me," I said, "but did you see a kid of about eleven in here this morning? He has dark, kind of thick hair, he's small, good and fat and walks with the one foot turned in?"

"Cheeky wee bugger," the man said, "told me to get a move on, him and his mate."

I couldn't resist it. It wasn't germane, but I had to know, "What did he order?"

"What did he not order? Ham and two eggs, black pudding, tomato, dip soda bread, beans, dip tatie bread – kept shouting 'More dip bread there waiter,' – finished up with a cream bun each, after all that."

I was nonplussed. He'd had the chance, but hadn't ordered a chop. But I thanked the man and went outside, content enough. It was now a quarter to one: they were due back for lunch any minute. I stood waiting, undressing the chops with my eyes.

It was three minutes to one by the clock on the far wall of the Burlington when wee Hughie turned up with Hector Scallion. "Hiya Sam. Coming in for some grub?"

I sighed. I'd expected it. Wee Hughie was all heart. Chances were I'd never get another chance to eat a complete chop as long as I lived, but I had to shake my head. I didn't want to be hauled into this. Although I knew that Uncle James was all talk, I didn't want even to be a thousand to one outsider to be tied to wee Hughie as he was tied to a tram.

"You're in it up to here," I told him. "I've been sent to bring you back. How much have you left of the fifteen pound twelve and eightpence?"

He pulled the money out of his pocket and we counted it

— one pound five and threepence short.

"What the divil did you do with it?" I was nonplussed. It had disappeared at the rate of five shillings an hour since he'd knocked the dough off. I hadn't thought it possible to go through money at that rate.

"We were round in funland," wee Hughie explained. He meant the slot machine funfair in North Street. "We've got a ten bob bet done at the horses as well," he said.

"What time's the off?" I was tensing up.

"Half one. Kempton Park. Novice hurdle. Two mile. Second favourite."

"It's a cert," Hector Scallion put in. I gave him the mackerel eye. He was the coldest stew in Tiger's Bay, scared to bet a cigarette card never mind ten bob on a horse.

"Right," I said to him, "hit the trail, mate. You're out of the big picture."

Hector shrugged philosophically. He'd had a great time. He headed off.

I was firmly in charge now, "We've got to think, not spend. Let's get round to the bookies."

The bet had been done in McAlevey's pitch not far away, round the corner from the Belfast Telegraph. We stood outside. I borrowed a paper from a big fellow in dungarees. The horse's name was Hypnotherapist.

"How do you say that?" I wanted to know.

"Dunno," wee Hughie said, "I just wrote it down and sent it in."

He'd backed the thing on the nose. I could feel the hair rise on the back of my neck. Ten bob. I had to say one thing for wee Hughie – he didn't know the meaning of fear.

In those days they didn't give out the course betting. The selection was five to two in the paper. If it touched, there'd be one pound fifteen shillings back. When the race went off wee Hughie was nonchalantly talking about whether Crusaders football team would win the Intermediate Cup final the next day. I pulled him by the sleeve. "Come on and we'll look at the grub in the Burlington."

Right enough, it was always guaranteed to get the juices going. They'd added a roast chicken to the dazzling display. It certainly shoved the first race at Kempton Park to the back of our minds. In fact I was thinking, looking at that chicken, that if I'd had the managing of the window, I'd have surrounded it with chops like the leading lady and the chorus. But eventually we knew it was Kismet time.

"Hey mister, what won the first at Kempton?" we asked a little old man who was leaving, sadly tearing up his docket.

"Something called Hypno The Rapist," he said.

My heart leapt up. I asked for his paper.

"Is that it?" I pointed to Hypnotherapist.

"That's it – Hypno The Rapist," the man said, "two to one favourite." We gave him sixpence for collecting the bet.

We were four shillings and threepence to the good. There was just a spurt of dust to mark the spot where we'd stood outside the bookies. We hit the Burlington so fast that we were sitting down before the door closed behind us.

"Yes," said the hairy man, "and what would you like?"

"Bring me a chop while I'm thinking about it," I said, "and make it snappy."

The Thin Man

They were lovely years when I was in my teens. All I needed was sixpence and I was in there with a chance of throwing the bookie onto the dole. Sixpence was easily got. Blow Kennedy, the storyteller, who lived in a hovel with a cat and a promiscuous alcoholic aunt, had a supply of the pinhole cards that were all the go for charity in those days. One of his aunt's clients had been found dead of methylated spirits on the floor of the hovel and Blow had found the pinhole cards in the pocket of the deceased before anybody else could. Each card had about thirty tiny squares.

My own preference was to stop people in the street and say, "Would you like to give for the band uniform, please? A penny a hole," offering a pin so that the donor might puncture the centre of a square for each penny given. This was supposed to reassure the donor that each square would only be used once. As a guarantee of fraud prevention it wasn't what you might call watertight.

"And what's the name of the band, sonny?"

You had to be careful with this one. People knew their stuff on bands and if you mentioned a local flute band you might be challenged to name the piccolo player. But years of practice had given me a good shade of the odds in this area. "Twenty Seventh Boys' Brigade Pipe Band," I would say.

"Oh yes, and which church is that?"

"Saint Columbus, Knock."

"My, my, you're a long way from home sonny, here on York Street."

And I would say, "I'm over visiting with my mammy, and I'm the top collector, mister. I've collected more than anybody in the BB, mister, so I have, and Captain Williamson says I'm a credit to the company, so he did."

"Well and I'm sure you are, son. The Boys' Brigade is a fine character-building organisation. Here's a penny, give me your pin and jolly good luck to you," and I would thank the man, telling myself that seeing the state of the going and the weight that my nag of the day was humping, I was going to need it. Blow Kennedy, lurking in a nearby shop doorway, would take the first penny collected and shove off and from there on in I was on my own. It was truly satisfying when the stake was wrung from the public and I could relax, take up my position outside the bookies and get down to work.

Because of my age I wasn't allowed inside the bookies, but the customers all knew me and they would take my bet in and bring the docket back out to me. Sixpence was the minimum that the bookie would take, but if it wasn't much to him it was plenty to me. An even money winner meant that I had a shilling and that was enough to call it a day, go on the town, buy five Woodbine for tuppence, dander down into the centre of Belfast, maybe buy a bowl of stew for tuppence, go to the pictures for another tuppence and there I was, with the original sixpence intact for the next day's racing and a day at the fleshpots under by belt. On such a day, I wouldn't have called the King my uncle.

One day, after a tiring trawl of the Antrim Road for pinhole subscriptions towards football jerseys and pants for St Stephen's Church Lads' Brigade football team, I dropped wearily to the ground outside the bookies, too burnt out even to open my copy of the *Racing and Football Outlook*, for money had been scarce and I'd worked hard and sore for my sixpence.

The exercise hadn't begun well. I'd stopped a member of the Select Vestry of my own church without recognising him. But he most certainly recognised me and he wanted to know why I was working the streets on behalf of St Stephen's CLB football team, when I was the regular right half for St Barnabas' CLB within my own church.

"You're either a superb sport or you're a chancer," the man said.

"Ah, sure where would we be without a sense of sportsmanship," I came back, but there could be repercussions – like a dunder across the side of the head if details reached my mother, for she was bringing us up steeped in the church.

For another thing, there was hardly any money about. It was the end of the Co quarter, a time dreaded by the working classes of Belfast, most of whom were in hock to the Belfast Co-Operative Society and were required to clear up arrears built up over the previous three months. To today's generation it might seem almost like Stone Age thinking, but up to the Fifties the Belfast hoi polloi were terrified of debt. The Co quarter deadline was met in almost every case.

In the Thirties a young wife who lived in Tiger's Bay went out in the early hours of the morning, walked into the Waterworks pond on the Cavehill Road and drowned herself and the baby in her arms because, unknown to her husband, she owed twenty pounds to moneylenders and hire purchase shops. Another housewife in the Oldpark district gassed herself for the sake of twelve pounds. A woman in Mackey Street near us went to jail for a month over a debt of ten pounds in 1930. She came back to the street only to learn that her punishment wasn't over, for those of her neighbours who didn't look down their noses at her as a jailbird were openly envious because she was just about the only woman in the area who wasn't any longer in debt.

I wasn't half a minute sitting drawing my breath outside the bookies when I was joined by a man of about thirty. He was thin, gaunt even, with sunken eyes and a haunted look about him. He was dressed half respectably though, in a navy suit kept pressed, even though it was shiny all over through being ironed without the damp cloth. Still, I only noted this with one per cent of my faculties; it was time to get down to cases.

I produced from my pocket a betting slip and carefully wrote my double on it, then I eyed the thin man. "Would you take that and do it for me?" I asked. He rose.

"Certainly," he said. He gave a sad little smile, "I hope you'll have better luck than I had."

I'd taken two of Gordon Richards' mounts in successive

races. They were favourites in the paper. In those days there was no such thing as letting the punters know the betting before the off: we just bet blind. The first one came in at the surprising price of three to one second favourite, with something out of the blue backed down to odds on. This raised my temperature because I now had two shillings travelling on to the next horse whose name was Prickett, I still remember.

"All right for you," my companion said, clearly happy for me. "I'm keeping my fingers crossed for you."

I, of course, was keeping everything crossed. I was annoyed and I told the thin man so.

"Two shillings is enough for me," I explained. "It's actually too much. I don't want to win a whole lot of money, I just want to double my stake and quit. I'm not ambitious. If I'd known that Richards was three to one I'd only have done the single bet and I'd be on my way down the town for a bowl of stew now and the pictures."

"I wish I was as easily fixed up," the thin man said and if the melancholy in his voice had been transferred to the stage he'd have had thousands in tears. We sat, both of us, putting the twenty five minutes in until the decisive next race and I explained to him in more detail my working philosophy − that it is better to aim low and get five Woodbine, a bowl of stew and a picture show, than to lift your sights and end up with nothing but the long walk home.

"Still," he said, "if this double gets up, you'll hardly give the extra over a shilling back to the bookie," and I laughed heartily at the idea.

"I'll go in and catch it for you," he said when the time came for the off. There was no dramatic announcement of the off made at that time. A little plywood shutter came down over the hole separating clerk and customer at the exact second of the time the race was supposed to start, and if that shutter had been made of steel it would have amputated fingers, so suddenly and decisively did it drop. Nor was the result called out when it was received: the clerk came out from behind the counter, as the crowd stood in silence; he climbed the steps, chalk in hand; rubbed the surface with the wet duster and wrote the result on the board. It was only with the first letter that the punters knew their fate. I sat tense with excitement, waiting. I heard the phone ring, heard the door open, felt the silence as all talk in the pitch stopped, then the sudden burst of sound and the thin man came rushing out. His eyes were shining, "You did it! Two to one. You've got six shillings!"

I sat in stunned silence on the step outside the bookies. I was unable to reply when the thin man asked me what I was going to do with my winnings. I genuinely didn't know.

"I'll go in and lift it for you," he said when it was time and I gave him the docket, coloured dark yellow like gold, with the feel of a Bank of England promissory note.

I was sitting thinking that I would give the thin man sixpence for bringing me luck, when all of a sudden there he was over me. I looked up. He was smiling and this time there was nothing sad about it. In all my life I've never seen a happier smile.

"Here, this is more your mark," he shouted and dropped

a single shilling in my lap.

Then, as I sat staring, there was just a little scuff in the packed dirt where he had once stood and he was away like a rat up a spout with my five shillings.

I got to my feet and went in pursuit but he was good. I saw him heading for Tiger's Bay and there were too many back entries there in the maze of narrow streets. The thin man had gone.

I stood there looking up my last entry, then I shrugged. It might have been worse: he could have absconded with the whole winnings. Turning, I made for the centre of Belfast and the place that sold the bowls of stew. I would wake up tomorrow with three Woodbine left out of the five I was going to buy, sixpence in my pocket and all the good of the stew building me into a man. It wasn't the worst day in the history of the world. And anyway, maybe the thin man was decent at heart. Sure for all that I knew, maybe it was the pressure of the Co quarter that drove him to his dreadful crime.

Knickers and Things

When I was fifteen Mother called me in off the street one Saturday afternoon.

"I was up in Charley Medley's shop getting my messages," she said, "and he told me that one of his customers, a woman living on Duncairn Gardens, owns a warehouse and she's looking for a boy to start serving his time . . . What are you screwing up your face for?"

"I wouldn't be any good in a warehouse," I protested, "it's all women, sitting at sewing machines stitching shirts and things."

"That's a wareroom, for goodness sake, not a warehouse."

"Well what kind of a warehouse is it then? I don't like the sound of it."

"No, you don't like the sound of anything connected with work, sure we all know that. This is the chance of a good job, serving your time." As usual, she couldn't keep up the scolding for long. Her voice softened, "Go and wash your face and hands, darling, brush your clothes, comb your hair and go up and see Miss Black. She'll be in all day. It's ten shillings a week."

Ten bob a week. That was the sickening part of it. It was

really good money. The house needed it. I would have to give it my best go. But something warned me that this wasn't a day that I was going to look back on with any kind of pleasure. Imagine working for a woman. Washed shining clean, I crawled like a snail unwillingly to Miss Black's house.

She was tall and had a flat chest. I noticed the flat chest first. Don't forget, I was fifteen going up to sixteen. She was about forty five, had good skin, wore no make-up and she wore a sensible woollen skirt, a sensible woollen jumper and flat-heeled, extremely sensible shoes. At the front door she looked me over with narrowed eyes.

"Charlie Medley spoke to my mother. Something about a job," I said.

She invited me in and seated me on the sofa while she took a chair by the table.

"You look respectable enough," she began, "but you'll have to wear your good clothes if you get the job."

"These are my good clothes," I told her with some relief. I didn't like her quiet assumption of superiority. To this day I don't like quiet assumptions of superiority. I got up to go, but she waved me back down again.

"Tell me this, how much change would I get back from a ten shilling note if I bought a cushion cover for three shillings and sixpence and a pair of silk stockings for five shillings and elevenpence?"

"Sevenpence," I said, before she'd finished the last word.

Her eyes widened and she nodded with approval.

"Spell stylographic," was her next question.

I hesitated. "Has it an i or a y?" I asked.

"Y," she said.

"Because I need to know," I busted out laughing.

Miss Black sat perplexed for a good ten seconds, then she caught on. But she didn't laugh.

"Did you work that out yourself?" she wanted to know.

I nodded modestly, then I spelt stylographic.

"Do they call you Sam or Samuel?" she asked.

I shuddered and put her right.

"Listen Sam," she said, "this job is in a wholesale drapery warehouse. The word stylographic is used in the trade as a code to display the price of the goods that we charge to the retail drapers. You'll notice that there are twelve letters in stylographic. So if you saw on a price ticket the letters LR stroke I, what price would that item be?"

"It would be forty seven shillings and elevenpence," I said after a bit of thought.

"Now listen, we have credit drapers who send customers to us to be suited. We give the goods to the customer, who repays it to the draper at so much a week." Her nose wrinkled at the idea of paying on the never-never. It was the only system that my mother had ever used.

"We obviously can't quote the trade price to such a customer. If the retailer's margin is one third of the final price and you have an article that a customer wants marked LR/I, what price would you quote to that customer?"

"Seventy two shillings," I said at once.

Miss Black stood up; she was smiling a wintry kind of smile. "I think you'll be suitable," she said. "Actually you were suitable before I asked that final question. You're very quick at figures, aren't you? How does that come?"

She spoke in refined tones and they came easily. The accent wasn't shoved on. As well as that, there was a Southern roll to the words. I was soon to learn that it was West Cork, flattened out just a bit by contact with the Belfast sound.

I shrugged my shoulders. "Nearly all my mates can count like that," I said. "In our school if you got your sums wrong you got hit." In addition to that there was the expertise gained from backing horses, calculating sixpenny stakes at odds like thirteen to eight, but I wasn't about to get into that.

"Start next Monday morning," Miss Black said, "nine o'clock till five, finish at one on Saturdays." She gave me directions to the warehouse, half way up Howard Street near the back of the City Hall. I left her and went back home.

"Nine to five and the half day on Saturday!" Mother was all smiles. Her face was shining with pleasure. "Imagine, our Sam's got a proper office job. And ten shillings a week too. You must have made a good impression."

Resigned, I got offside and went up the park with Butler Forsythe to throw stones for chestnuts.

"I have a sinking feeling about this job," I told him.

"Well give it to me then," Butler said, "ten bob a week? I would commit murder every day for ten bob a week."

"You couldn't do it with your stutter, sure you know that." Butler could talk freely to his mates, but in front of a stranger his voice took a wobbler. It had taken him six months to relax when he was placing a bet.

On Monday morning I turned up for work at ten to nine. In five minutes another guy of about seventeen arrived.

"Are you the new boy?" he asked.

I nodded, weighing him up. He didn't look too bad: fair wavy hair, a bit pansy, but with a friendly smile. He had a very good suit on compared to my navy blue shiny job. Mine was too tight for me as well. No wonder. It had been new when I'd been confirmed by the Bishop two years earlier, the year that Tiberius won the Ascot Gold Cup. The other guy's name was Teddy Kelly.

"What kind of a job is it?" I asked.

"It's all right at times," he said, "but at other times it's bloody awful. Mister Black's all right mostly, but Maisie, she's mustard. You'll soon see."

With that they both arrived. The brother was a long drink of water, with a drip at the end of his sharp nose, a heavy overcoat, a pullover and a woollen muffler round his neck although it was only a crisp autumn day outside. He paid very little attention to me. Inside my eyes widened in disbelief. Under a glass roof, the place was tiny. Some warehouse: Bobby Kennedy's betting shop near Castle Junction was bigger. Rows of ladies' coats and suits hung on stands around two sides of the room. Boxes on shelves lined the four walls, and satin cushion covers and sideboard runners were on display on tables by the door.

The two Blacks went at once to a tiny office alcove and began to check over some book-work, calling out figures aloud. I followed Teddy through a door to a small narrow yard. He produced a large tin of salmon-pink, disinfectant-smelling sawdust labelled Dustall, two soft floor brushes with their bristles covered with cloth and handed one of the brushes to me. God, how I came to detest the smell of that Dustall. Forever after, I associated the job with the smell. It was our first job each morning after we'd taken the covers off the coat racks, to spread the stuff over the brown lino, scrub it in with the brush until there wasn't a single bacterial organism left alive in the place and then use the other brush to polish the lino to a high shine. It was women's work, like everything else in that awful place.

It was on that first morning that I experienced the special talents of the Blacks for inflicting torture on the working class. As the Assembly Hall clock chimed ten, Miss Black summoned me. "Go across the road to the cafe and tell them you're from Black's," she said. In the cafe I was attended to by a waitress in a black dress and lace apron and dainty cap. On a wooden tray she placed a pot of tea, four slices of fresh toast, two hot muffins and a tiny pot of jam. As I carried that tray across Howard Street, the smell rising up from it sent my digestive juices racing and jumping mad. By the time I laid it in front of the Blacks I was having a job to keep from slavering.

"Thank you Sam," said Miss Black. "Now go and tidy up."

Teddy and I retired behind one of the coat stands and there we brushed the shoulders of the coats or we straightened the boxes or set the cushion covers in line as we listened to our bosses enjoy their morning break.

"Mmm David, I was ready for that, weren't you?"

"Yes, indeed Maisie, the toast's lovely, isn't it?"

Champ, champ, crunch, crunch, nibble, nibble. Teddy and I hid out of sight behind the stand like two characters out of

Dickens, with our stomachs roaring.

"Care for some jam on that muffin, David?"

"Do you know Maisie, I think I will. It's just delightful, isn't it?"

Behind the stand I was about ready to rip the leather belt off a high-collared coat and devour it whole.

The first morning went in like a month. At half past twelve it was lunch time. I walked the mile to Hillman Street and attacked the heated-up Sunday broth, spuds and boiling meat like somebody just off a hunger strike. Then I walked back, dreading the hours ahead, feeling so frustrated that I almost cried. That torture was to last nine long months.

I had been there a week when Miss Black said to Teddy Kelly, "Now I think Sam has been here long enough to attend to the customers by himself. Let him serve the next one to come in." She turned to me, "You do a five year apprenticeship in this business, so you might as well start now."

If this was supposed to please me, it was well off the mark. There was no way I was going to get worked up about drapery as a trade. To be born and reared within sight and sound of three shipyards, the term apprenticeship meant a real trade – shipwright, engineer, the sort of training that fitted a man to go to sea. That's what I'd always wanted to do, like my father and brother, but both Mother and Dad were against it.

"It's a rough dirty life," was Mother's view. "I want to see you in a real nice job." Well, here I was in just the job and it was putting me astray in the bloody mind.

The next customer to come in was a little, stout,

comfortable lady. Teddy whispered that she owned a draper's shop in Comber, County Down, then he pushed me towards her.

"What was it you wanted?" I asked, in anything but a real shop assistant's tone, but Teddy was behind, putting me right.

"Good morning Mrs Moles, how can we help you?" he said. Then he moved back: I was on my own, going solo. Her next words sent me into a tail spin.

"I would like to see some slip and knicker sets," she said.

I just stood looking at the woman, as if I was Butler Forsythe and Mrs Moles was Fairy Feet the cop.

"Pardon?" I got it out weakly. I was still having trouble in taking in what I had just heard.

"Slip and knicker sets, for dear sake," she said. "I want to see your slip and knicker sets, boy."

God in heaven look down on me this day, how on earth could I ever face the lads at the corner if this news got out? I'd told them it was in a warehouse so they were imagining something like a shed at the docks, an acceptable kind of a job. But this? It conjured up a nightmare. "Hey Sam, is it true that you sell knickers?" This could finish me as a fighting force in Tiger's Bay. I would probably have to leave town, never to return.

"What's the problem?" Oh no, now Miss Black was on the job.

"I only wanted to see some slip and knicker sets," said Mrs Moles from Comber, bewildered at the sight of an open-mouthed youth before her turned to a pillar of stone. I was impatiently elbowed aside, Miss Black produced some boxes and handed them to me.

"There you are Mrs Moles. Sam, do you think you could possibly carry on from here? He's new, Mrs Moles, just started. Sorry."

As if it was happening to someone else, I saw my hand take the lid off, exposing coral satin knickers with frilly edges, folded and sitting neatly on top of a matching slip.

Mrs Moles shook her head, "Hold them up."

I nearly told everybody in the warehouse to stuff the job, then I remembered the ten bob a week and Mother's smiling face.

But, as the makers of Epsom salts would say, everything passes. In time I grew hardened. The knickers news never did get out and I slipped somehow into a way of working.

Each day I walked the mile home and back twice and as I walked, I used to look for signs from heaven that the end of my dreadful ordeal was near, that the incessant nagging and girning from Miss Black and her big jinny brother David would fade and die. At traffic lights I would say, "If I can reach the other side before the lights turn yellow, it'll mean rescue." It wasn't a fifteen-year old lad crossing the road then — I was a blur.

But relief was bound to come and when it did, it was at a time when my spirits were at their lowest. It was late summer, time to show the firm's autumn samples around the retail drapers. Teddy was delighted to explain the procedure because he no longer had to do it now that he was the senior boy. It involved the greatest loss of face I had ever suffered in my life, or ever will. No wonder Teddy was glad to be shot of it. Drippy Nose David was too timid to drive a car and too stingy to hire a driver, so he hired a handcart instead. And guess who was down to push it, with a the huge hamper of samples on top. It was something that I couldn't bring myself to mention to anybody; not the lads at the corner, certainly not Mother.

The procedure was that Mr Black would take the tram to the shop and wait for me to arrive. Over the next two weeks I pushed that blasted handcart up the Ormeau Road, the Newtownards Road, the Ravenhill Road, the Cregagh Road and just about every main road in the city of Belfast, all the time dreading the time when I would have to push it along York Street, my own familiar ground.

There was no way that I could explain away pushing a handcart. Only ragmen and dealers of low degree pushed handcarts, not trainee managers of wholesale warehouses, which was the title I had managed to bestow on myself at the street corner. But inevitably York Street's time had to come and come it did. For the ordeal I donned a duncher cap, pulled it down over my eyes and even walked with one shoulder low and a pronounced limp as I entered my home territory. I walked with my eyes down, my head turned away from the pavement and, by the time I reached the first call, I thought I'd got away with it. David was waiting impatiently. I opened up the hamper, he grabbed a handful of samples and was just turning to go into the shop when a voice called:

"Hey boy, what are you doing with a handcart?"

I turned; so did Mr Black. It was my Uncle Thomas.

Somehow, the minute I saw him and saw the look on his face, I knew that at last I was going to be free.

Uncle Thomas was a dock labourer, a hard lick: small, but made of indiarubber. He was standing in his working clothes staring, pushing his cap to the back of his head.

"What the hell's gates are you doing with the handcart?"

Mr Black, his arms full of jumpers, skirts and blouses, stopped. His mouth fell open.

"It's part of the job," I said.

"Part of the job?" Uncle Thomas turned to Mr Black and gave him a push that sent him half across the pavement. "What the hell d'ye think ye've got here, a bloody horse? We didn't send this lad out of a good decent home to push a bloody handcart. What kind of a job is this anyway? Answer me. Are you his boss?"

There was no way that Mr Black could answer. His eyes were like banjos and he kept wildly looking around as though for help from Maisie, the strong one.

"Yes," I said treacherously, sliding a whinge into my tone, "he's the boss and he told me to push this. I've been at it all week, so I have."

By the second, my hopes were rising. I knew Uncle Thomas. He was going to get really active in a matter of seconds. There could be nothing but good news in it for me. Meanwhile Mr Black was standing paralysed. Then suddenly he did exactly the right thing, from my point of view. He found his voice.

"How dare you!" he squeaked. "I'll get the authorities on you, pushing me like that."

"Pushing you?" Uncle Thomas took his cap off, doubled it and shoved it into his jacket. Music filled my soul. Over the sound of the trams, the motor cars and the shipyard clatter, I heard a lark sing in the clear air. Mr Black was about to be duffed up.

He was pushed again, this time good. His tie was pulled out, the garments went flying all over the pavement, he was pinned against the wall and, with Uncle Thomas's face a half inch from his own, he was given a very severe talking to.

"D'ye see that lad there, well he has more brains in his big toe than you have in your whole long string of a body, ya girnin' ghost, ye. We all thought that he was in a good job. Not one of us knew that you were working him like a donkey. Get over there, get a houl o' them shafts and take that bloody cart back to wherever it came from."

He propelled Mr Black between the shafts, gathered up the goods from the pavement and, with his two hands, shoved man and handcart along the road.

"Get you away up home," he shouted to me, taking his cap out and putting it back on top of his head. "Tell yer mother that I told you not to go back. Imagine, a McAughtry, pushing a frigging handcart . . . "

Shaking his head, he went off along York Street.

I didn't walk home that day – I danced home. Next morning I went down to the boys' labour exchange in Alfred Street.

"I missed you," the clerk said, getting my file out. "Now let's see if we can't get you another job along the same lines."

"If that's meant to be a joke," I said, "it's in very poor taste."

Saving Dock Ward
for the Union

*T*he first time I ever got mixed up in party politics was in
the Stormont election of 1938, when the Labour man and
sitting member for Dock Ward, Harry Midgley, who up until then had had the support of both sides, found himself in
a tough fight against two opponents, one of whom was Tony
Clarke, later Sir George Clarke, Bart.

In our street they were all Tony Clarke mad. Not only was
he the Official Unionist candidate, but his family were said
to own a shipyard, which placed him about fifty jumps above
us in the social scale. He was an extremely good-looking
young man, slim, with golden hair, and he went in for yellow
or powder blue roll-neck pullovers. The local Protestant mill
and factory girls simply doted on him. So did the older Prod
women, come to that, including my own mother. I remember
her remarking that there was one thing about Tony Clarke,
he always looked very clean compared to the men of our
street.

The third candidate in the Dock Ward election was General
Franco, currently leading the insurgents in the Spanish Civil
War. The general was too busy to come over to Hillman Street
and the New Lodge Road and Sailortown to fight the seat

in person, so the Catholic Church, which went the bundle on Franco at that time, encouraged a Nationalist Jim Collins to stand.

This would split the Catholic vote and make sure that Harry Midgley lost the seat, in order to teach him a lesson for picking the wrong side. He was against General Franco.

Harry, who was chairman of the Northern Ireland Labour Party at that time, was Stormont's leading advocate for the poor and until war broke out in Spain he was enormously popular with both traditions. But alas, he had given aid and comfort to some anti-Franco officers of two Spanish merchant ships which were lying in the Port of Belfast, impounded for the want of harbour dues. And better than that, he engaged in open debate with priests of the Roman Catholic Church on the Spanish Civil War and made no bones about his opposition to the General. The whole place in consequence was in an uproar.

In Dock Ward we talked of little else. We had hardly a rag on our backs, we were living on champ and broth made from a tuppenny bone, we'd hardly shoes to our feet, we were queueing up for stale loaves and there we were running around worrying about the Spanish Civil War. Belfast Celtic had won the Irish Cup for the second year running, but they needn't have bothered because the next morning, throughout the whole of Catholic territory, the newspaper billboards read: "Franco Wins Stunning Victory in Catalonia."

When the evening of polling day came and with only an hour left to vote, there came the usual and well-loved panic. Unionist Party workers rushed out of the tally rooms and began to shout loudly, "It's looking bad, the Nationalists are winning, everybody out!".

I happened to be bouncing a ball at the corner of the street, trying to hit a halfpenny on the ground. Standing watching me was Chuck Jepson, over on holiday from Chicago and staying with relations in Meadow Street. Every cell and corpuscle in me was conditioned by birth and upbringing to respond on the instant to calls from Official Unionist tally rooms.

"I'm away to knock doors," I said to Chuck Jepson, shoving the ball in my pocket and breathing hard. Being half Unionist and half American, one half of Chuck wanted to run like hell for Ulster and the other half wanted money for doing it. He negotiated a fee of sixpence from the Unionists. I pointed to Meadow Street.

"You take the far side and I'll take the near one," I said and away I went as if from starting blocks. But Chuck stopped me with a shout.

"What are we supposed to be doing?" he wanted to know.

"We knock doors and shout to whoever comes out that it's looking bad, the Nationalists are winning and everybody out. What do you think we're supposed to be doing."

As was customary on such occasions, the streets in Dock Ward were black with people zigzagging back and forward, going excitedly from house to house. Invalids were being helped downstairs to inch painfully to the polling stations, mothers wrapped shawls around their children and themselves and hirpled up the street in their gutties to vote.

The people of Dock Ward were enjoying themselves immensely.

To raise the temperature to fever level, out came our own candidate – God bless him – taking time away from being a gentleman to come and actually meet us, shake hands and talk to us. Tony Clarke had also brought along some of his own sort as well, young men who owned motor cars and upper-class girls who could actually drive them. They were all urging a maximum turnout. I happened to whizz up to them on my door-knocking duties and a gorgeous girl in a yellow summer dress smiled at me and said, "How is it going?"

Stuck for words, I gaped for a second. I didn't want to let our street down. This girl would expect a highly sophisticated answer. I remembered the billboards.

"We'll need to watch ourselves. I see where Franco had a stunning victory at Casablanca," I said.

The girl stared then, laughing, gave me a little push. "Keep up the good work." Her accent was English. She spoke the way that the girls did in the pictures. Away I went, hopelessly in love.

Of course, the sense of emergency was heightened by the clear evidence across the Border, by Trainfield Street and Lepper Street and the New Lodge Road, of frantic activity on the part of the Nationalists. They were showing every bit as much excitement as ourselves. I remember standing there thinking that it was marvellous, the sheer magnificent challenge of that final flying hour before polling finished. It came as quite a disappointment when the peelers, under the

101

head constable with the steel plate in his head from a war wound, took the boxes away in the Black Maria. In the hiatus that followed the end of polling, I suddenly missed Chuck Jepson.

I began to search the crowd standing outside the Unionist tally rooms. Dear knows he shouldn't have been hard to pick out for he wore the most ridiculous pair of knickerbocker trousers, and as if that wasn't daft enough, he had on top of his head one of those dinky little white US Navy hats. I used to think that the American kids had necks like brass, going around in outfits like that. For myself, I preferred short trousers, bare knees, socks to the ankles, one of our Tommy's shirts with the collar stitched up to make it fit my pipestem of a neck and a skull-cap to top off the ensemble.

But there wasn't a sign of a knickerbocker. I began to worry. This was Chuck Jepson's first Dock Ward election. There were rules of engagement to be followed, otherwise things could be tricky. Then just with that I spotted him.

He was coming into view in the distance, from the direction of the New Lodge Road, travelling at a rate of knots and only just ahead of a sizeable posse of Nationalist kids. I ran to Checkpoint Charlie, located at Spamount Street, yelling for the Yank — for there wasn't much more than the space of a flying tackle between him and the nearest of his pursuers. The closer he came to safety, the faster they moved, until the whole lot were running in a blur. But Chuck Jepson made it across the Border by a short length.

"What the divil were you doing over there?" I asked when his breathing had come back to normal.

"Knocking doors and shouting. You told me to go to the far side, didn't you?"

"God in heaven take care of us all," I whispered, "you weren't over in the New Lodge Road shouting 'It's looking bad, the Nationalists are winning, everybody out' were you?"

He nodded, "The whole way up it."

Seemingly Chuck had left so much disbelief behind him as the Nationalist kids had tried to reconcile the first part of his message with the second that actual pursuit hadn't commenced until he'd crossed his own track on his way home.

It was a near thing and I'm sure Chuck Jepson kept the kids in his part of Chicago enthralled with his story when he got back to the States again. I can just imagine him saying, "A week's supposed to be a long time in politics, but you should have seen the length of that two minutes when they were chasing me."

Tony Clarke beat the Nationalist and poor Harry Midgley came trailing in third, beaten out of sight. There was cheering and celebrations by both Unionists and Nationalists when the result was announced at the City Hall next day, for both sides had done what they'd set out to do. The Unionists had won the seat from Labour and General Franco had stuffed Harry Midgley.

"If that Yankee mate of yours hadn't wakened them up over there, we'd have won by a bigger margin," one of the Unionists complained after the shouting had died down.

"That's the gloomy side of it," I replied. "Look at it this way. After Chuck Jepson's solo door-knocking effort last night, they'll all be thinking that their part of Dock Ward is riddled with secret Unionist voters. We've unnerved them, mate."

Thinking back on it now, mind you, it's quite possible that one of that chasing posse was Gerry Fitt, now Lord Fitt, who was to take Dock Ward from the Unionists, hold it for donkey's years and make a complete liar out of me. Funny old world, isn't it?

The Fight Game

My cousin Jim Kernaghan was a great guy. He was good-looking, well built, big-hearted, athletic and it was no surprise in our circles when, at the age of seventeen, he took up the fight game.

Nowadays we are used to fighters starting off in the amateur ranks, learning the business gradually under the guidance of wise and compassionate teachers and then moving into the professional ring after proving that they have the skills to make headway in that more demanding field. But fifty years ago and more well over half of those active in pro boxing came into the game without ever having been in an amateur ring.

Jim Kernaghan took up boxing because he had his eye blacked by a big ignorant haymaker at the corner of our street and Jim thought it was time to look into the reasons why that swing was allowed to land and to make certain sure that it wouldn't happen again.

He was taken on by a man who ran a boxing club in the evenings and sold fruit from a pony cart during the day. The club was called the Conlon Club and it occupied an empty two-up, two-down house on the Oldpark Road in Belfast. I used to go there to watch Jim's preparation, but I didn't take part myself. By then I had discovered that, although I was well able to look after myself in a street fight, I was a complete poultice in the ring.

There are obvious differences in the two forms of fighting. The preliminaries in the ring involve due and formal warning that a fight is about to start, thus giving both fighters an equal chance. But controlled boxing also ensures that, as far as possible, two men of comparable weight and ability are matched. This is far from the case in street fighting, where you would need your head examined if you were to start a war without some kind of telling advantage. I was like a matchstick man when I was a young lad and consequently I was often challenged to combat. The fact that I sang in the robed choir in church and had to walk through one of the toughest districts in Belfast wearing a bow tie and stiff Eton collar didn't do anything to give me a quieter life. Hence, a controlled start to a murdering match was the last thing I wanted.

What I used to do was to whine and plead for mercy and when the other guy started to turn away in disgust at my cowardice I whaled him, aiming for the button of the jaw in order to make sure that he was too fuzzy to protect himself from the two-fisted onslaught that was to follow. Yet I longed with all my heart to be a champion boxer, to part my short haircut in the middle, to have a slightly flat nose and to walk with short half-running steps and my elbows out. But after half a dozen fights in the ring at the Ministry of Labour Juvenile School in Alfred Street, where unemployed kids had

106

to go in order to qualify for the dole, it was clear that it was not to be. Crying and whining and surprise attacks are not allowed in the ring.

So when Jim Kernaghan took up the game, I was delighted. I could be a part of the whole process from novice to title-holder without having to take a single dig myself. At the same time, if our neighbourhood chose to believe that my close connection with boxing meant that I was a boxer too, well, it wasn't up to me to put them right.

It was marvellous when, under the name of Jack Kernaghan, he started off by putting other novices to bye-byes. In those pre-war times there were boxing arenas all over Belfast. I sat cheering Jim to victory in the Chapel Fields, the ring in Thomas Street, the Harp's Hall and the Ulster Hall. It was in the last-named, one evening in early 1939 that Jim had his last pro fight.

He was eighteen, he'd beaten a dozen or so novices, but then he was stopped in six rounds by Barney Wilson, a punishing body-puncher, one of the best of our local welter-weights. It was agreed that he'd met Barney's class of scrapper too soon; Jim took a new manager, a man from a North Queen Street boxing family, and was soon matched with a lad called Patterson from Lisburn in eight two-minute rounds at the Ulster Hall.

It was a punishing scrap. Both fighters had good left leads and soon their faces began to show it. There was very little in it until, halfway through the fight, the Lisburn scrapper landed a solid right in Jim's solar plexus.

He went down onto one knee, was over the effects at six,

looked to his corner for instructions, stayed down on his chief second's signal and was counted out, as fit as a fiddle.

Afterwards in the dressing room I consoled my cousin as he got himself together. The whole inside of his mouth was a mass of tiny cuts from his opponent's lefts. Patterson, sharing the dressing room, had taken every bit as much punishment, but he'd been using a proper gumshield whereas poor Jim, who'd lost his gumshield somewhere and couldn't afford another, had fought using orange peel. As the fight progressed, the orange peel had been pulverised. Jim had had to swallow it before it choked him and after the fourth round his second had peeled another orange and replaced it.

When he was dressed we set off in search of Ma Copley the formidable promoter, a legend in boxing. We found her in the dressing room used by the top of the bill Tommy Armour, a welterweight with the most deadly left hand in British boxing. They were arguing about money even though Armour was stripped and due in the ring.

Ma Copley won the argument, the stars of the evening began their walk to the ringside and Jim asked for his purse.

"Who are you?" she asked.

"Second on the bill," Jim told her.

She buried her hand in a heavy leather bag that hung by a strap from her shoulders, pulled out a fistful of silver, counted out eight half crowns and dropped them in Jim's hands.

A pound was well below what had been expected but, after the way Ma Copley had handled a daughty warrior like Tommy Armour, Jim was in no mood to argue. We made our way to the corridor, where Jim's manager was waiting for his half crown commission. As we were leaving by the front door, a man appeared on the pavement outside, announced that he was the manager's brother and that it was the done thing to see him right as well, so another half crown took a walk. That left fifteen shillings. We walked along the quiet street.

"Could have taken him, you know," Jim said.

"I know that all right. Money for jam."

"I was well over that dig."

"Sure I know. That guy in your corner must have been full drunk. Maybe you could get a rematch," I suggested.

Jim was quiet for a while, then: "To tell you the truth, I'm thinking of joining the Air Force," he said, "they're looking for men." They were indeed. It was after Munich and working its way up to Poland.

"You'll win the Air Force Championship," I told him.

Up past Clifton Street I said, "Fancy a fish supper?"

"OK." Jim produced another half crown. "Get some smokes as well," he said.

"Plenty of salt and vinegar," I told the woman in the chippie through force of habit. We hurried up the last few hundred yards to get to Jim's house on the Oldpark Road while the fish supper was still warm.

"I promised my Mammy ten shillings out of the purse," Jim told me on the way. "I thought I'd have been getting more than a quid."

Jim's father had a bad stomach from the First War. He was upstairs sleeping. Jim's mother my Aunt Lena, all worried frowns and ringlets, rushed to make us tea when we arrived. She gave the fish supper a bit of a boost in front of the fire as the tea was drawing, then she set us up to the table with the fish and chips on proper plates and bread and marge alongside it. When she sat down to watch us, in the way that mothers do, Jim put four half crowns in her hand. She smiled all over her face, looked at the clock, kissed him and rushed out to the wee shop at the corner to get eggs and bacon for the family for the next morning's breakfast.

Jim took a forkful of chips, shoved them in his mouth and immediately half rose from his seat, his face screwed up in agony, as the vinegar and salt struck. He spat the chips out and threw them into the fire. When he got his senses back he pushed his plate of fish and chips over to me and sat, drawing healing air into and around his mouth. Gratefully I waded in. In no time at all I had polished off the lot. When Aunt Lena came back she said, "Well, are you feeling better now son?"

Jim nodded. "Great," he said.

Later, with his mother upstairs and feeling nice and well-fed, I lit up a Players and said to Jim, "So. That's your last pro fight, eh?"

He nodded, working his stinging mouth, closing his eyes every so often with the discomfort.

"With the money you gave to the manager and his brother, the ten bob to your mother and the half crown for the smokes and the fish suppers, that leaves you with half a crown and a busted mouth. You're left with one eighth of the purse and you couldn't even eat the fish supper. You didn't win the fight because your second can't count, yet you're sitting there

110

and never a complaint out of you. Tell me this . . . "

"Tell you what?" he asked. A little smile was trying to fight its way past the smarting of his lips. I had always amused Jim by the way I took events and worked them, as if over a furnace.

"If you had it all to do again, would you still do the same?"
He shook his head. I was satisfied.

"What way would you play it?" I asked.

"I would play it this way," he said, rubbing his solar plexus where the dig hand landed and lisping on the sibilants. "Know when you got the fish suppers? Well, I would have told you to take it easy on the salt and vinegar."

Testimony at Portrush

I was up in Portrush on the north coast of Antrim for the weekend. I was ready for a rest. My eyes, tired from squinting through binoculars at slow horses on windy days, were half open – one half resting and the other half lamping a big number sunbathing a yard away, dressed only in three twisted hankies. It was a glorious summer's day marked by the shrill cries of gulls and the even shriller cries of the people at the end of their bombing run. The wife was in Portrush town looking round the shops. Finally, I closed my eyes altogether. The girl had turned over showing her back. Backs are nothing. I lay letting the sun do its healing work, allowing my thoughts to drift in the usual direction.

I had just reached the point where I had called the family together and was saying to my three daughters, "What I'm going to do is this: instead of handing you £80,000 each out of my pools win, I'm going to clear your mortgages and give you the balance of the £80,000. How's that? That'll still leave me two million."

"Oh Daddy, you're wonderful!"

"I know. Toddle off now, your mother and I wish to study the Rolls Royce brochure."

"God bless you Daddy. You're a saint."

"Not for a while yet, I hope."

. . . Suddenly I opened my eyes and sat up. The peace was being murdered by a group of evangelists. They had a public address system that would have done for a Bruce Springsteen gig in the grounds of Shane Castle.

Three hundred holidaymakers sat bolt upright, trembling with shock. Any dreams they'd had about winning the pools were in splindereens. Now they knew where they were all right: they were in Portrush – evangelists' country, land of the reedy hymn singer, the Coolmore Gallops of the preaching fraternity.

The noise of the singers almost blanked out the blat-blat of a low-flying helicopter hovering over a group of people at one end of the strand. They were being photographed; they were objects of suspicion because they didn't have Protestant noses.

There were to be four preachers. It was easy to see it. They were standing with their eyes shut, practising their lines.

The music stopped and the first of them stepped forward.

"I was a sinner."

The public address system sent the message swirling, dipping and diving as far as Portstewart a couple of miles up the road.

"I was a gambler." The words were flung like mortar bombs.

"I threw away my hard-earned money on the horses."

"I was a destroyer. Now I've seen the light . . ." His voice was strong. The other preachers-in-waiting smiled, happy in the knowledge that they too would fight the good fight when their turns came. Their eyes narrowed, as they rehearsed their testimonies.

"The bookie got most of my money." Like any evangelist worth the name, he closed his eyes tightly and jabbed a forefinger at the sky as he spoke. It came as a distinct surprise, therefore, when he opened his eyes and found that he had someone alongside him at the head of affairs: I was that man.

It surprised me too, but there I was, smiling politely, dusting sand off my hands. I reached out courteously, gesturing towards the mike and uncertainly it was surrendered. I blew into the mike then asked, "What kind of a bet was it that dropped you in it?"

Giving him no time to answer, I went on, "Ladies and gentlemen, it was because of a two hundred quid bet on Razeem, favourite for the Derby, that I was driven to seek peace on the sands of Portrush." I could feel the crowd's sympathy growing for me. "Honestly," I went on and even the helicopter seemed to dip lower, listening, "I had already backed it at fours so I stiffened it with another big one at fives."

In the audience, heads were shaking. "My dear good people," I finished with a tremor in my voice, "they're out looking for Razeem yet. It is somewhere along the back straight at Epsom, a Marie Celeste among horses, drifting rudderless, leaving me ruined."

The sudden sob of a woman was heard. With a sad smile, as thunderous applause broke out, I handed the mike back to the evangelist.

He took my hand. Tears glistened in his eyes.

"I'm crying," he said into the microphone, "I'm crying for another sinner. Poor bastard . . . I mean . . . Poor chap." He paused, fighting his emotions then "My testimony's the same, only it was a hurdler name of Tobago that did for me." The holidaymakers were tense, listening.

"I had two hundred on it at nine to four on. A field of twelve broke evenly. They galloped at a cracking pace for the first. And it was at the first obstacle, ladies and gentlemen, that Tobago fell."

The helicopter's blattering was no match for the spontaneous cry of sympathy that was wrung from the crowd.

"By the holy sailor," a County Derry voice cried, "Isn't that always the way? It's the nicest punters that get the biggest hidings. The ones that win are the ones that wouldn't give ye the skin of their spit, never mind set up a pint."

"It's a shame," a Belfastman in the front row shouted. His nose was quite button-shaped. From the helicopter a soldier leaned out and photographed it.

By now the line of evangelists was rippling restlessly. Suddenly the line broke. A gentle looking girl, slightly built with dark hair to her shoulders, grabbed the mike just as the first preacher was breathing in.

"I was a sinner too," she announced in a low ladylike voice, "I once took Mother's dress without telling her, to go to a dance. . . . "

"Wheel her off," the crowd yelled, "we want real sinners."

Biting her lip, the girl stepped back into line.

A third evangelist decided to have a go. He was short, had

a shock of red hair and his trousers were a couple of inches above his shoes.

"I was a desperate sinner," he shouted in a Ballymena accent, "I once ordered a pint, gave the barman a fiver, got change back for a tenner and I stuck the extra in my pocket without saying anything."

The speaker blushed with pleasure as the holidaymakers cheered him to the echo, but before he could cash in on the punchy opening a little fat, elderly man leapt up from a kneeling position and took the mike.

"I was once chinned for a five-timer by a Vincent O'Brien three-year-old," he shouted. "Lost a hundred and ten and what do you think I did?"

"Blew your brains out and ruined your pants," somebody yelled. The man smiled good-naturedly as raucous laughter rang out. He shook his head.

"No," he said, "instead I went straight into McGlone's bar, cashed a bouncer for fifty quid and got full drunk for three days. During the afternoon of the third day I got three doubles and a treble up, it paid my seventy quid. I paid off the dud cheque and changed my ways completely. Now I follow Dermot Weld instead of Vincent O'Brien." Under his crown of shining white hair, the kindly face glowed with pleasure as the audience gave him a standing ovation.

It was against this background that the fourth and last preacher, a middle-aged, tall, thin man, soberly dressed, stepped up. The noise fell to an expectant hush. This speaker had all the outward and visible signs of a proper preacher. He put a hand in his pocket with practised ease, took it out again, raised the same hand until there was no sound to be heard except the protests by a group of snub-nosed visitors as they were taken away to Castlereagh for questioning.

"My friends," the preacher began. The crowd readied itself for a prayer. "My friends, I have here in my hand two old halfpennies. These coins, some of you will recall, were the sort that were once used for the gambling game known as pitch and toss . . . "

There was a feeling amongst the crowd of a good day well spent. It was time to end the proceedings in the usual way. They got ready for the Benediction and a hymn after this little sermon on the evils of gambling was over.

"Do you remember pitch and toss?" the tall man said.

They all yelled, "Yes."

"OK," replied the preacher, "then I'll bet any one of yez I'll head them. I'll take all sizes and shapes of money up to fifty quid. Come on lads, form a circle there. Fifty quid says I'll head them. Hurry up now . . ."

As he finished, the choir began to sing, "I'm h.a.p.p.y, I'm h.a.p.p.y, I know I am, I'm sure I am, I'm h.a.p.p..y."

". . . Hurry up will you?" I opened my eyes. The hanky girl had gone; the wife had returned. She was leaning over me shouting. I sat up, "What's the matter?"

"What do you think?" She had to yell to make herself heard.

"I'm h.a.p.p.y, I'm h.a.p.p.y . . . " right in front of us a group of evangelists were singing their heads off. All around sunbathers were sitting up, rubbing their eyes.

"Come on, it's time for a cup of tea."

117

The first preacher took the microphone. He was a clean-cut lad about twenty. He wore a Queen's University graduate's tie.

"Good afternoon everybody," he said, "isn't it a lovely day. In keeping with it we'd just like to sing a hymn called *Above The Clear Blue Sky*."

The religious interlude promised to be pleasant enough. But it wouldn't be half as riveting as the dream.

I looked up at the clear blue sky, gathered up my things and began to move off. At about five hundred feet a helicopter sat surveying the scene. Not that it bothered me any. With my nose, the product of hundreds of years of Protestant breeding, I was OK.